Packing My Library

Yale UNIVERSITY PRESS   NEW HAVEN AND LONDON

Alberto Manguel

PACKING MY LIBRARY

$$\left\{ \begin{array}{c} An \\ Elegy \\ and \\ Ten \\ Digressions \end{array} \right\}$$

Yale University Press books may be purchased in quantity for
educational, business, or promotional use. For information, please
e-mail sales.press@yale.edu (U.S. office) or sales@yaleup.co.uk
(U.K. office).

Designed by Nancy Ovedovitz and set in Palatino and
Weiss Bold types by Integrated Publishing Solutions.
Printed in the United States of America.

Library of Congress Control Number: 2017950992
ISBN 978-0-300-21933-3 (hardcover : alk. paper)

A catalogue record for this book is available from the British Library.

This paper meets the requirements of ANSI/NISO Z39.48-1992
(Permanence of Paper).

10 9 8 7 6 5 4 3 2 1

For Craig

A man would have no pleasure in
discovering all the beauties of the
universe, even in heaven itself, unless
he had a partner with whom he
might share his joys.

—Cicero, *De amicitia*, 88

Packing My Library

My last library was in France, housed in an old stone presbytery south of the Loire Valley, in a quiet village of fewer than ten houses. My partner and I chose the place because next to the house itself was a barn, partly torn down centuries ago, large enough to accommodate my library, which by then had grown to thirty-five thousand books. I thought that once the books found their place, I would find mine. I was to be proved wrong.

I knew I wanted to live in this house the first time I opened the heavy oak carriage doors that led across the entrance into the garden. The view, framed by the arched stone portal, was of two ancient *Sophora* trees casting shadows over a soft lawn that stretched all the way to a distant gray wall; we were told that underground, vaulted corridors had been dug out during the peasant wars to connect the house with a now crumbling tower in the distance. Over the years, my partner cared for the garden, planted rosebushes and a vegetable plot, and tended to the trees, which had been savagely treated by the previous owners, who had filled one of the hollow trunks with garbage and allowed the top branches to become dangerously fragile. Every time we walked through the garden we spoke of being its guardians, never its owners, because (as with all gardens) the place felt possessed by an independent spirit which the ancients called numinous. Pliny, explaining the numinosity of gardens, says that this is because at one time trees were the temples of the gods, and the gods had not forgotten. The fruit trees in the back corner of the garden had grown over an abandoned cemetery dating back to the ninth century; perhaps here too the ancient gods felt at home.

The walled garden was an extraordinarily quiet place. Every morning at about six, I would come downstairs, still half-asleep, make myself a pot of tea in the dark rafted kitchen, and sit with our dog on the stone bench outside to watch the morning light creep along the back wall. Then I would go with her into my tower, which was attached to the barn, and read. Only the song of birds (and in summer, the drone of honeybees) broke the silence. In the evening twilight, tiny bats flew around in circles, and at dawn the owls in the church steeple (we never understood why they chose to build their nest under the toll-ing bells) swooped down to catch their supper. They were barn owls, but on New Year's Eve a huge white owl, like the angel that Dante describes steering the ship of souls to the shores of Purgatory, would glide noiselessly across the dark.

The ancient barn, whose stones carried the signature of their fifteenth-century masons, housed my books for almost fifteen years. Under a ceiling of weathered beams, I gathered the survivors of many previous libraries from my childhood on. I had only a few books that a serious bibliophile would have found worthy: an illuminated Bible from a thirteenth-century German scriptorium (a gift from the novelist Yehuda Elberg), an Inquisitor's manual from the sixteenth century, a number of contem-porary artist's books, quite a few rare first editions, and many signed copies. But I lacked (still lack today) the funds or the knowledge to become a professional collec-tor. In my library, shiny young Penguins sat happily side by side with severe-looking leather-bound patriarchs. The books most valuable to me were private association copies, such as one of the earliest books I read, a 1930s edition of Grimms' *Fairy Tales* printed in somber Gothic type. Many years later, memories of my childhood drifted back whenever I turned the yellowed pages.

I set up my library according to my own requirements and prejudices. Unlike a public library, mine demanded no common codes that other readers could understand and share. A certain zany logic governed its geography. Its major sections were determined by the language in which the books were written: that is to say, without distinction of genre, all books written originally in Spanish or French, English or Arabic (the latter a language which I can't speak or read) sat together on a shelf. I allowed myself, however, many exceptions. Certain subjects—the history of the book, biblical commentaries, the legend of Faust, Renaissance literature and philosophy, gay studies, medieval bestiaries—had separate sections. Certain authors and certain genres were privileged: I collected thousands of detective novels but very few spy stories, more Plato than Aristotle, the complete works of Zola and hardly any Maupassant, all of John Hawkes and Cynthia Ozick but barely any of the authors on the *New York Times* best-seller list. I had on the shelves dozens of very bad books which I didn't throw away in case I ever needed an example of a book I thought was bad. Balzac, in *Cousin Pons,* offered a justification for this obsessive behavior: "An obsession is a pleasure that has attained the status of an idea."

Though I knew that we were only the keepers of the garden and the house, the books themselves, I felt, belonged to me, were part of who I was. We speak of certain people who are reluctant to lend an ear or a hand; I seldom lent a book. If I wanted someone to read a certain volume, I'd buy a copy and offer it as a gift. I believe that to lend a book is an incitement to theft. The public library of one of my schools carried a warning both exclusionary and generous: "THESE ARE NOT YOUR BOOKS: THEY BELONG TO EVERYONE." No such sign could be put up in my library. My library was to me an utterly private space that both enclosed and mirrored me.

When I was a child in Israel, where my father was the Argentine ambassador, I was often taken to play in a park that started off as a well-kept garden and faded into sandy dunes. Huge tortoises plodded their way across it, leaving dainty tracks in the sand. Once I found a tortoise whose shell had been half torn off. It seemed to stare at me with its ancient eyes, as it dragged itself over the dunes towards the sea beyond, bereft of something that had protected and defined it.

I've often felt that my library explained who I was, gave me a shifting self that transformed itself constantly throughout the years. And yet, in spite of this, my relationship to libraries has always been an odd one. I love the space of a library. I love the public buildings that stand like emblems of the identity a society chooses for itself, imposing or unobtrusive, intimidating or familiar. I love the endless rows of books whose titles I try to make out in their vertical script that has to be read (I've never discovered why) from top to bottom in English and Italian, and from bottom to top in German and Spanish. I love the muffled sounds, the pensive silence, the hushed glow of the lamps (especially if they are made of green glass), the desks polished by the elbows of generations of readers, the smell of dust and paper and leather, or the newer ones of plasticized desktops and caramel-scented cleaning products. I love the all-seeing eye of the information desk and the sibylline solicitude of the librarians. I love the catalogues, especially the old card drawers (wherever they survive) with their typed or scribbled offerings. When I'm in a library, any library, I have the sense of being translated into a purely verbal dimension by a conjuring trick I've never quite understood. I know that my full, true story is there, somewhere on the shelves, and all I need is time and the chance to find it. I never do. My story remains elusive because it is never the definitive story.

Partly this is because I can't think in a straight line. I digress. I feel incapable of going from factual starting points across a neat grid of logical stepping-stones to a satisfying resolution. However strong my initial intention, I get lost on the way. I stop to admire a quotation or listen to an anecdote; I become distracted by questions that are alien to my purpose, and I'm carried away by a flow of associated ideas. I begin by talking about one thing and end up talking about another. I tell myself that I'll consider, for instance, the subject of libraries, and the image of the ordered library conjures up in my disordered mind unexpected and haphazard holdings. I think "library," and I'm immediately struck by the paradox that a library undermines whatever order it might possess, with random pairings and casual fraternities, and that if I, instead of sticking to the conventional alphabetical, numerical, or thematic path that a library puts forward for my guidance, allowed myself to be tempted by non-elective affinities, my subject would become no longer the library but the joyful chaos of the world the library intends to put in order. Ariadne transformed for Theseus the labyrinth into a clear-cut and simple path; my mind transforms the simple path into a labyrinth.

Borges observed in an early essay that a translation can be understood as equivalent to a draft, and that the only difference between a translation and an early version of a text is merely chronological, not hierarchical: where the draft precedes the original, the translation follows it. "To suppose that any recombination of elements is necessarily inferior to its original," wrote Borges, "is to suppose that draft 9 is necessarily inferior to draft H, since there can be nothing but drafts. The concept of a *definitive text* belongs only to religion or to fatigue." Like Borges's text, I have no definitive biography. My story changes from library to library, or from the draft of one library to the next, never one precisely, never the last.

One of my earliest memories (I must have been two or three at the time) is of a shelf full of books on the wall above my cot from which my nurse would choose a bedtime story. This was my first personal library; when I learned to read by myself a year or so later, the shelf, transferred now to safe ground level, became my private domain. I remember arranging and rearranging my books according to secret rules that I invented for myself: all the Golden Books series had to be grouped together, the fat collections of fairy tales were not allowed to touch the minuscule Beatrix Potters, stuffed animals could not sit on the same shelf as the books. I told myself that if these rules were upset, terrible things would happen. Superstition and the art of libraries are tightly entwined.

That first library stood in a house in Tel Aviv; my next library grew in Buenos Aires, during the decade of my adolescence. Before returning to Argentina, my father had asked his secretary to buy enough books to fill the shelves of his library in our new house; obligingly, she ordered cartloads of volumes from a secondhand dealer in Buenos Aires but found, when trying to place them on the shelves, that many of them wouldn't fit. Undaunted, she had them trimmed down to size and then re-bound in deep-green leather, a color which, combined with the dark oak, lent the place the atmosphere of a glade. I pilfered books from that library to stock my own, which covered three of the walls in my bedroom. Reading these circumcised books required the extra effort of supplanting the missing bit of every page, an exercise that no doubt trained me to read later the "cut-up" novels of William Burroughs.

After this came the library of my adolescence, which, built throughout my high school years, contained almost every book that still matters to me today. Generous teachers, passionate booksellers, friends for whom giving a book was a supreme act of intimacy and trust helped me build it. Their ghosts kindly haunted my shelves, and the books they gave me still carry their voices, so that now, when I open Isak Dinesen's *Gothic Tales* or Blas de Otero's early poems, I have the impression not of reading the book myself but of being read to out loud. This is one of the reasons I've never felt alone in my library.

I left most of these early books behind when I set off for Europe in 1969, sometime before the military dictatorship in Argentina. I suppose that had I stayed, like so many of my friends, I would have had to destroy my library for fear of the police, since in those terrible days one could be accused of subversion merely for being seen with a book that looked suspicious (someone I knew was arrested as a Communist for carrying Stendhal's *The Red and the Black*). Argentinian plumbers found that there was an unprecedented call for their services, since many readers tried to burn their books in their toilet bowls, causing the porcelain to crack.

In every place I settled, a library began to grow as if by spontaneous generation. In Paris and in London and in Milan, in the humid heat of Tahiti, where I worked as a publisher for five long years (my Melville novels still show traces of Polynesian mold), in Toronto and in Calgary, I collected books, and then, when the time came to leave, I packed them up in boxes and forced them to wait as patiently as possible inside tomblike storage spaces in the uncertain hope of resurrection. Every time I would ask myself how it had come to pass: how this exuberant jungle of paper and ink had entered yet another period of hibernation, and if, once again, it would cover my walls like ivy.

My library, either settled on shelves or packed away in boxes, has never been a single beast but is a composite of many others, a fantastic creature made up of the several libraries built up and then abandoned, over and over again, throughout my life. I can't remember a time in which I did not have a library of some sort. My libraries are each a sort of multi-layered autobiography, every book holding the moment in which I read it for the first time. The scribbles in the margins, the occasional date on the flyleaf, the faded bus ticket marking a page for a reason today mysterious—all attempt to remind me of who I was then. For the most part, they fail. My memory is less interested in me than in my books, and I find it easier to remember the story read once, long ago, than the young man who was its reader.

My earliest public library was that of Saint Andrews Scots School, one of the several elementary schools I attended in Buenos Aires before the age of twelve. It had been founded as a bilingual school in 1838 and was the oldest school of British origin in South America. The library, though small, was for me a rich, adventurous place. I felt like a Rider Haggard explorer in the dark forest of stacks that had a earthy smell in summer and reeked of damp wood in winter. I would go to the library mainly to put my name on the list for the new Hardy Boys installment or a collection of Sherlock Holmes stories. That school library, as far as I was aware, didn't have a rigorous order: I would find books on dinosaurs next to several copies of *Black Beauty*, and war adventures coupled with biographies of English poets. This flock of books, gathered with no other purpose (it seemed) than to offer the students a generous variety, suited my temperament: I didn't want a strict guided tour, I wanted the freedom of the city, like that honor (we learned in history class) that mayors bestowed in the Middle Ages on foreign visitors.

I've always loved public libraries but I must confess to a paradox: I don't feel at ease working in one. I'm too impatient. I don't like to wait for the books I want, something that is unavoidable unless the library is blessed with the generosity of open stacks. I don't like being forbidden to write in the margins of the books I borrow. I don't like having to give back the books if I discover in them something astonishing or precious. Like a greedy looter, I want the books I read to be mine.

Perhaps that is why I'm not comfortable in a virtual library: you cannot truly possess a ghost (though the ghost can possess you). I want the materiality of verbal things, the solid presence of the book, the shape, the size, the texture. I understand the convenience of immaterial books and the importance they have in a twenty-first-century society, but to me they have the quality of platonic relationships. Perhaps that is why I feel so deeply the loss of the books that my hands knew so well. I'm like Thomas, wanting to touch in order to believe.

First Digression

All our plurals are ultimately singular. What is it then that drives us from the fortress of our self to seek the company and conversation of other beings who mirror us endlessly in the strange world in which we live? The Platonic myth about the original humans having a double nature that was later divided in two by the gods explains up to a point our search: we are wistfully looking for our lost half. And yet, handshakes and embraces, academic debates and contact sports are never enough to break through our conviction of individuality. Our bodies are burkas shielding us from the rest of humankind, and there is no need for Simeon Stylites to climb to the top of a column in the desert to feel himself isolated from his fellows. We are condemned to singularity.

Every new technology, however, offers another hope of reunion. Cave murals gathered our ancestors around them to discuss collective memories of mammoth hunts; clay tablets and papyrus rolls allowed them to converse with the distant and the dead. Johannes Gutenberg created the illusion that we are not unique and that every copy of the *Quixote* is the same as every other (a trick which has never quite convinced most of its readers). Huddled together in front of our television sets, we witnessed Neil Armstrong's first step onto the moon, and, not content with being part of that countless contemplative crowd, we dreamt up new devices that collect imaginary friends to whom we confide our most dangerous secrets and for whom we post our most intimate portraits. At no moment of day or night are we inaccessible: we have made ourselves available to others in our sleep, at mealtimes, during travel, on the toilet, while making love. We have reinvented the all-seeing eye of God. The silent friendship of the moon is no longer ours, as it was Virgil's, and we have dismissed the sessions of sweet silent thought which Shakespeare enjoyed. Only through old acquaintances popping up on Facebook do we summon up remembrance of things past. Lovers can no longer be absent, or acquaintances long gone: at the flick of a finger we can reach them, and they can reach us. We suffer from the contrary of agoraphobia: we have become haunted by a constant presence. Everyone is always here.

This anxiety of being surrounded by the words and faces of others permeates all our histories. In Petronius's Rome, Encolpius wanders through a museum looking at the images of the gods in their amorous entanglements and realizes that he is not the only one to feel the pangs of love. In China, in the eighth century, Du Fu wrote that an old scholar sees in his books the populous universe that whirls around him like an autumn wind. Al-Mutanabbi, in the tenth century, likened his paper and pen to the entire world: to the desert and its traps, to war and its harsh blows. Petrarch doesn't possess his library as much as his library possesses him. "I'm haunted by an inexhaustible passion that up to now I have not managed or wanted to quench. I feel that I have never enough books," he says. "Books delight one in depth, run through our veins, advise us and bind with us in a kind of active and keen familiarity; and an individual book does not insinuate itself alone into our spirit, but leads the way for many more, and thus provokes in us a longing for others." Goethe's Werther, on the contrary, wants only one book: his Homer, which is, he says, a *Wiegengesang*, a lullaby to soothe him. For Pushkin's Tatyana, Eugene Onegin's books are what she requires to reflect back her erotic passion. For Jules Verne's Captain Nemo, his library holds the only human voices that deserve to be spared from destruction. In every one of these cases, the individual is obsessed with finding others who will tell him or her who they are. As if we were Heisenberg's electrons, we feel as though we don't always exist: we exist only when we interact with someone else, when someone else deigns to see us. Perhaps, as quantum physics teaches us, what we call reality—what we think we are and what we think the world is—is nothing but interaction.

But even interaction must have its limits. The fifth edition of the DSM (the *Diagnostic and Statistical Manual of Mental Disorders*), published in 2013 by the American Psychiatric Association, lists "Internet Gaming Disorder" as a pathology that leads to "clinical significant impairment or distress." What Mariana in the Moated Grange might have called melancholy, and what Doctor Faust calls "a burning of the heart" the DSM calls "depression associated to withdrawal" (when the technology breaks down) and "a sense of unfulfillment" (when it fails to deliver). The end result is the same.

The search for others—to text, to email, to Skype, or to play with—establishes our own identities. We are, or we become, because someone acknowledges our presence. The motto of the electronic age is Bishop Berkeley's "esse est percipi," "to be is to be perceived." And yet, all the crowds of friends promised by Facebook, all the multitudes of correspondents wanting to link across cyberspace, all the merchants of promise who offer fortunes in foreign lands, partners in virtual orgies, penis and breast enlargements, sweeter dreams and better lives cannot remedy the essential spleen for which Plato imagined his story.

"After intercourse all animals are sad," Aristotle (or perhaps Galen) is supposed to have said, and to have added: "except the rooster, who then sings." Aristotle was referring to sexual intercourse. Perhaps all intercourse—with pictures, with books, with people, with the virtual inhabitants of cyberspace—breeds sadness because it reminds us that, in the end, we are alone.

I WOULD ARGUE THAT PUBLIC LIBRARIES, HOLDING both virtual and material texts, are an essential instrument to counter loneliness. I would defend their place as society's memory and experience. I would say that without public libraries, and without a conscious understanding of their role, a society of the written word is doomed to oblivion. I realize how petty, how egotistical it seems, this longing to own the books I borrow. I believe that theft is reprehensible, and yet countless times I've had to dredge up all the moral stamina I could find not to pocket a desired volume. Polonius echoed my thoughts precisely when he told his son, "Neither a borrower nor a lender be." My own library carried this reminder clearly posted.

I love public libraries, and they are the first places I

visit whenever I'm in a city I don't know. But I can work happily only in my own private library, with my own books—or, rather, with the books I know to be mine. Maybe there's a certain ancient fidelity in this, a sort of curmudgeonly domesticity, a more conservative trait in my nature than my anarchic youth would have ever admitted. My library was my tortoise shell.

Sometime in 1931, Walter Benjamin wrote a short and now famous essay about readers' relationship to their books. He called it "Unpacking My Library: A Speech on Collecting," and he used the occasion of pulling his almost two thousand books out of their boxes to muse on the privileges and responsibilities of a reader. Benjamin was moving from the house he had shared with his wife until their acrimonious divorce the previous year to a small furnished apartment in which he would live alone, he said, for the first time in his life, "like an adult." Benjamin was then "at the threshold of forty and without property, position, home or assets." It might not be entirely mistaken to see his meditation on books as a counterpoise to the breakup of his marriage.

Packing and unpacking are two sides of the same impulse, and both lend meaning to moments of chaos. "Thus is the existence of the collector," wrote Benjamin, "dialectically pulled between the poles of disorder and order." He might have added: or packing and unpacking.

Unpacking, as Benjamin realized, is essentially an expansive and untidy activity. Freed from their bounds, the books spill onto the floor or pile up in unsteady columns, waiting for the places that will later be assigned to them. In this waiting period, before the new order has been established, they exist in a tangle of synchronicities and remembrances, forming sudden and unexpected alliances or parting from each other incongruously. Lifelong enemies Gabriel García Márquez and Mario Vargas Llosa for instance, will sit amicably on the same expectant shelf while the many members of the Bloomsbury group will find themselves each exiled to a different "negatively charged region" (as the physicists call it) waiting for the wishful reunion of their particles.

The unpacking of books, perhaps because it is essentially chaotic, is a creative act, and as in every creative act the materials employed lose in the process their individual nature: they become part of something different, something that encompasses and at the same time transforms them. In the act of setting up a library, the books lifted out of their boxes and about to be placed on a shelf shed their original identities and acquire new ones through random associations, preconceived allotments, or authoritarian labels. Many times I've found that a book I once held in my hands becomes another when assigned its position in my library. This is anarchy under the appearance of order. My copy of *A Journey to the Center of the Earth*, read for the first time many decades ago, became in its alphabetically ordered section a stern companion of Vercors and Verlaine, ranking higher than Marguerite Yourcenar and Zola, but lower than Stendhal and Nathalie Sarraute, all members of the conventional fraternity of French-Language Literature. No doubt Verne's adventurous novel retained in its pages traces of my anxiety-ridden adolescence and of one long-vanished summer in which I promised myself a visit to the Sneffels volcano, but these became, once the book was placed on the shelf, secondary features overruled by the category to which the language of its author and the initial of the surname have consigned it. My memory retains the order and classification of my remembered library and performs the rituals as if the physical place still existed. I still keep the key to a door that I will never open again.

Places that seem essential to us resist even material destruction. When in 587 B.C.E. Nebuchadnezzar set fire to the First Temple in Jerusalem, the priests gathered with the keys to the sanctuary, climbed to the burning roof, and cried out, "Master of the World, since we have not merited to be trustworthy custodians, let the keys be given back to you!" They then threw the keys toward heaven. It is told that a hand came out and caught them, after which the priests threw themselves into the all-consuming flames. After the destruction of the Second Temple by Titus in 70 C.E., the Jews continued to perform the holy rites as if the ancient walls still rose around them, and they kept on reciting the prescribed prayers at the times that their corresponding offerings had been performed in the vanished sanctuary. And ever since the destruction, a prayer for the building of a third Temple has been a formal part of the thrice-daily Jewish service. Loss entails hope as well as remembrance.

Because a library is a place of memory, as Benjamin noted, the unpacking of one's books quickly becomes a mnemonic ritual. "Not thoughts," Benjamin writes, "but images, memories," are conjured in the process. Memories of the cities in which he found his treasures, memories of the auction rooms in which he bought several of them, memories of the past rooms in which his books were kept. The book I take out of the box to which it was consigned, in the brief moment before I give it its rightful place turns suddenly in my hands into a token, a keepsake, a relic, a piece of DNA from which an entire body can be rebuilt.

Second Digression

One night, one of the many nights of lying feverish in bed, breathless and coughing blood, the thirty-eight-year-old Robert Louis Stevenson dreamt of a terrifying hue of brown. Since his early childhood, Stevenson had depicted his frequent night terrors as "visits from the Night Hag," which only the voice of his nanny could calm with Scottish folktales and songs. But the Night Hag's hauntings proved persistent, and Stevenson found that he could turn them to his advantage by exorcising them through words. The awful color brown in his nightmare was thus transformed into a story. This, he tells us, was how the tale of Dr Jekyll and Mr Hyde was born.

Writers are just as astonished as their readers at the existence of successful literary creations. A few of these moments of conception have come down to us. The story of the would-be knight in search of justice occurred to Cervantes, he tells us, while he was languishing unjustly in prison; the story of the tragic consequences of dreaming up a life for Madame Bovary occurred to Flaubert after he read a snippet in a newspaper. Bradbury explains that the first stirrings of the dreadful world of *Fahrenheit 451* came to him in the early 1950s after seeing a couple walking hand in hand down a Los Angeles sidewalk, each with one ear plugged into a portable radio.

And yet, in most cases, the moment of literary creation is as unknown to us as that of the universe itself. We can study every fraction of a second after the Big Bang as we can read (in the days when writers kept their early scribbles) every draft of *À la recherche du temps perdu* or the various versions of Auden's poems. But the moment of birth of most of our best-beloved books is more mysterious. What sparked the first idea for the *Odyssey* in the mind of the poet or poets we call Homer? How did a storyteller who didn't care to sign his or her name dream up the atrocious story of Oedipus that was later to inspire Sophocles and Cocteau? What sad lover of flesh and hot blood lent his character to the irresistible figure of Don Juan, damned for all eternity?

Authorial confessions seldom sound truthful. Edgar Allan Poe explained in a lengthy essay that "The Raven" was born from his intention to write a poem on what he judged "unquestionably, the most poetical topic in the world," the death of a beautiful woman, and to use for its refrain the most resonant syllables in the English language, "er" and "ore." The words *never more* immediately suggested themselves for the refrain, and in order to allow them to be repeated he chose not a person but a bird that could speak them. He didn't choose a parrot, which in his opinion was not poetic enough (he was right), but a raven, appropriate to his gloomy soul. Poe's explanation is logical, cleverly presented, and entirely unbelievable.

Perhaps we should content ourselves with admitting that miracles are possible, without asking how. Everything that can be imagined proves in the end to come into being somehow: everything, from perfect creations like *Orlando Furioso* or *King Lear* to perfect abominations, such as land mines or electric prods. And because we still believe in cause and effect, we demand an explanation for everything: we want to know how each thing came to be, what made it happen, what was the first heartbeat that set the beast in motion, where did this thing that now stands before us come from.

Fortunately for us, fortunately for the survival of the human intelligence, abominations can be explained, though perhaps too late for remedy, by historical and psychological analyses. Fortunately as well, literary creations cannot. We can find out what authors say about the circumstances surrounding the act of creation, what books they read, what were the everyday minutiae of their life, the state of their health, the color of their dreams. Everything, except the instant in which the words appeared, luminous and distinct, in the poet's mind, and the hand began to write.

I REMEMBER THAT ON THE FIRST DAY I BEGAN setting up my library in France, I took out of its box a first edition of Kingsley's *Hypatia*, a novel about the fourth-century philosopher and mathematician who was murdered by Christian fanatics. I remember opening the book and coming upon the description of the Library of Alexandria, a passage I had completely forgotten except for the words "rainless blue," without recalling where they came from. This was the passage: "On the left of the garden stretched the lofty eastern front of the Museum itself, with its picture galleries, halls of statuary, dining-halls, and lecture-rooms; one huge wing containing that famous library, founded by the father of Philadelphus, which held in the time of Seneca, even after the destruction of a great

part of it in Caesar's siege, four hundred thousand manuscripts. There it towered up, the wonder of the world,
its white roof bright against the rainless blue; and beyond
it, among the ridges and pediments of noble buildings, a
broad glimpse of the bright blue sea."

How could Kingsley's description have slipped my
mind as I was trying to depict Alexandria and its library
in a book I wrote a few years later? Why was my memory not more helpful when I was painfully trying to piece
together an image, factual or imaginary, of what the ancient library might have been? My mind is capricious.
Sometimes it can be charitable: in moments when I need
a consoling or happy thought it throws at me, like coins
to a beggar, the alms of an event that I had long forgotten,
a face, a word from the past, a story read one sultry night
between the sheets, a poem discovered in an anthology
that my adolescent self believed no one had discovered
before. But the generosity of my books is always there,
as part of their makeup, and as I took them out of their
boxes, having condemned them to silence for so long,
they still were kind to me.

As I unpacked my books on the remote afternoon that
restored Kingsley's passage to me, the empty library
started to fill with disembodied words and the ghosts of
people I knew once, who had guided me through libraries
vaster than that of Alexandria. The unpacking also conjured up images of my own younger self at different times:

carefree, brave, ambitious, solitary, arrogant, all-knowing; disappointed, bewildered, somewhat afraid, alone and aware of my ignorance. Here were the magic talismans. Here was a paperback with selections from Tennyson in which at the age of twelve I first read "Tithonus," underlining the words I didn't understand before learning the poem by heart. Here was Lucretius's *De rerum natura* full of penciled annotations from my Latin class. Here was a Spanish translation of Clausewitz's *On War* that had belonged to my father, bound in green leather and trimmed of its first lines. Here was H. G. Wells's *The Island of Doctor Moreau*, which my friend Lenny Fagin gave me for my tenth birthday. Here was the edition of the *Quixote* edited by my beloved professor Isaias Lerner and published by the University Press of Buenos Aires, which was later shut down by the military authorities who forced Lerner into exile. Here was the copy of Kipling's *Stalky & Co.* that Borges had read in his adolescence in Switzerland and which he gave to me as a parting gift when I left for Europe in 1969. Here was Louis Hémon's *Maria Chapdelaine*, which had belonged to the Canadian businessman Timothy Eaton and whose pages had been cut only to page 93, with a bookmark from the Savoy Hotel in London—a book that symbolized for me my adopted country: the quintessential Quebecois novel written by a Frenchman, read halfway through by an Anglo-Canadian magnate in an aristocratic London hotel. Such encounters occurred many times during the happy months I spent among the piles of disinterred volumes.

Packing, on the contrary, is an exercise in oblivion. It is like playing a film backwards, consigning visible narratives and a methodical reality to the regions of the distant and unseen, a voluntary forgetting. It is also the reestablishment of another order, albeit secret. "Bonding" (as physicists call this process of new chemical formations) entails the clustering of unlikely items into groups and identities redefined through the new boundaries of a boxed cartography. If unpacking a library is a wild act of rebirth, packing it is a tidy entombment before the seemingly final judgment. Instead of the boisterous, endless columns of resurrected books about to be awarded a place according to private virtues and whimsical vices, their grouping is now established by a nameless common grave that transforms their world from the loud two dimensions of a shelf to the three dimensions of a carton.

The library in France was packed by several generous friends who descended like good spirits to help us overcome our reluctance. Lucie Pabel and Gottwalt Pankow arrived from Hamburg; Jillian Tomm and Ramón de Elía from Montreal and stayed at the house cataloguing the books, mapping their layout, wrapping them and placing them in cartons. They in turn summoned other friends, who came and helped for weeks at a time, until all the books were gone from the shelves and the library was transformed into a roomful of building blocks gathered in the midst of empty stacks. When the *Mona Lisa* was stolen from the Louvre in 1911, crowds came to stare at the bare space with the four pegs that had held the painting, as if the absence carried meaning. Standing in my empty library I felt the weight of that absence to an almost unbearable degree.

After the library was packed and the movers came and the boxes were shipped off to their storage place in Montreal, I would hear the books calling out to me in my sleep. "I am not resigned to the shutting away of loving hearts in the hard ground," wrote Edna St. Vincent Millay. "Gently they go, the beautiful, the tender, the kind; / Quietly they go, the intelligent, the witty, the brave. / I know. But I do not approve. And I am not resigned."

There can be no resignation for me in the act of packing a library. Climbing up and down the ladder to reach the books to be boxed, removing knick-knacks and pictures that stand like votive figures before them, taking each volume off the shelf, tucking it away in its paper shroud are melancholy, reflective gestures that have something of a long good-bye. The dismantled rows about to disappear, condemned to exist (if they still exist) in the untrustworthy domain of my memory, become phantom clues to a private conundrum. Unpacking the books, I was not much concerned with making sense of the memories or putting them into a coherent order. But packing them, I felt that I had to figure out, as in one of my detective stories, who was responsible for this dismembered corpse, what exactly brought on its death. In Kafka's *The Trial*, after Josef K. is placed under arrest for a never-specified crime, his landlady tells him that his ordeal seems to her "like something scholarly which I don't understand, but which one doesn't have to understand either." "Etwas Gelehrtes," Kafka writes: something scholarly. This was what the inscrutable mechanics behind the loss of my library seemed to me.

But I needn't dwell on how it came to pass. For reasons I don't wish to recall because they belong to the realm of sordid bureaucracy, in the summer of 2015 we decided to leave France and the library we had built there. It was the absurd conclusion to a long and happy chapter and the start of another that, I hardly dared hope, would be equally happy and at least as long. After the inane circumstances that forced us to go, taking down the library felt like a counterbalancing act similar to that of Benjamin after his divorce. Packing the books was, as I said, a premature burial, and I now had to endure the consequent period of anger and mourning.

Here I should explain that I'm not a seeker of novelty and excitement. I take comfort not in adventures but in routine. I enjoy, especially now as I'm approaching seventy, the moments when I don't have to reflect on everyday actions. I like to walk through a room with my eyes shut, knowing through habit where everything is. In my reading as in my life, I don't care much for surprises. Even as a boy, I remember dreading the moment in a story when the hero's happy days would be interrupted by an unexpected and terrible event. Though I knew from my other books that there would be a resolution, most often satisfying, I wanted to dwell on the brief first pages in which Dorothy lives peacefully with her aunt and uncle, and Alice has not yet started her fall down the rabbit hole. Because my childhood was largely nomadic, I liked to read about settled lives running their ordinary course. And yet, I was aware that without disruption there would be no adventure. Perhaps this idea was colored by the presumption that disruptions—misfortunes, injustices, calamities, suffering—are the necessary conditions for literary invention. "The gods weave misfortunes for men," King Alcinous says in the *Odyssey*, "so that the generations to come will have something to sing about." I wanted the song but not the tapestry.

Third Digression

The notion that misery is at the root of the creative process has its origins in a fragment ascribed to Aristotle, or,
rather, to Aristotle's school. Throughout the centuries, this
melancholic notion acquired both positive and negative connotations and was explored by relating it to somatic causes,
psychic inclinations, and spiritual choices, or as a reaction
to certain natural or cultural environments. The variety
of such ascriptions is indicative of melancholia's lasting
attraction. From Aristotle on (and probably long before),
philosophers, artists, psychologists, and theologians have
attempted to find in the almost indefinable state of melancholia the source of the creative impulse, and even perhaps

that of thought itself. Being melancholic, sad, depressed, unhappy (as popular belief has it) is good for an artist. Misery, they say, produces good art.

This belief implies two corollaries, more dangerous still. The first is that there is an existential state in which we are not miserable. Not satisfied with the story that once, in Eden, we were happy and now we have to earn our bread with the sweat of our brow, we are surrounded by ads that tell us that we can reach Eden again with the help of a platinum credit card and look as beautiful as the first Eve with the assistance of a fashion designer. The second implied belief is that art is somehow to blame for making us unhappy. The Controller in Aldous Huxley's *Brave New World* succinctly justifies the decision to eliminate art from human society: "That's the price we have to pay for stability. You've got to choose between happiness and what people used to call high art. We've sacrificed the high art."

Of course, leaving aside the fact that our emotions are wonderfully kaleidoscopic, it would be truer to say that it is in a happy state that artists work best. Schopenhauer's existential despair and physical agony were only alleviated in the moment of writing, and whether he felt suddenly happy and wrote, or started to write and felt suddenly happy, no one will ever know. We can tell that Dante, in his gloomy exile, had moments of happiness when in the course of the poem he meets Casella on the beach of Purgatory or Brunetto Latini on the burning sands of Hell, and we can suppose that out of the memory of the blissful past came the poem, in spite of what Francesca has to say about remembered joys.

Philip Larkin has a poem, "None of the books have time," in which he describes these two emotional states, one melancholic, empathetic to suffering, the other ego-centered, blissfully oblivious to the pain of the world. The myth that the artist needs suffering to create tells the story the wrong way round. Suffering, no doubt, is the human lot, and poems describe that suffering. However, the song comes afterwards, not in the writhing of misery but in the recollection of that misery and the respite from it provided by the writing.

A century ago, Thomas Carlyle described the writer in these words: "He, with his copy-rights and his copy-wrongs, in his squalid garret, in his rusty coat; ruling (for this is what he does), from his grave, after death, whole nations and generations who would, or would not, give him bread while living." More than likely, as we all know, they would not.

So there he or she sits, at a small table, staring at a blank wall or at a wall covered with bits and pieces, cards and photos and cartoons and memorable sayings, like the wall of a prison cell from which there's no escape. On the table, the tools of the trade. They used to be pen and paper, or a rickety typewriter, but of course now it's the word processor, whose screen, until just a few years ago, gave off an eerie green glow like kryptonite, draining this superman, or superwoman, of strength. What else is on the table? A collection of totemic figures that are supposed to bring luck and ward off the evil spirits of distraction, of sloth, of procrastination—magical objects to guard against the curse of the icy blank spaces. An empty cup of tea or coffee. A stack of unpaid bills. Where did this pathetic image of the writer come from?

In Greece and Rome there were, on occasion, writers who appeared lonely and penurious, like the cynic Diogenes in his barrel or the poet Ovid exiled to the slums of Toomis. But they were specific cases, miserable because of specific circumstances, because they chose to live with none of the modern comforts, like Diogenes, or because they were punished for speaking the truth, like Ovid.

Perhaps it was in the Middle Ages that the image of the poor scribe came into being: fingers gnarled with cold, cramped in his high chair, bent over his parchment, eyes straining to catch the feeble light. Wherever this image might have sprung from, the fact is that it stuck. The writer in the corner, the writer far from the madding crowd. And of course, the writer poor. Virtuous poverty, a notion that early Christians shared with the Greek Stoics, is of the essence. In the popular imagination, poverty and the suffering of the flesh allowed communion with the Holy Spirit or the muse.

It is useless to counter that hundreds and thousands of writers don't conform to these lugubrious criteria. There are the writers of the road, like the Provençal poets or Jack Kerouac. There are the gregarious writers, like André Malraux or F. Scott Fitzgerald. There are the writers rolling in money (admittedly fewer than in the previous categories), like Somerset Maugham or Nora Roberts. But the image has been seeded and it has taken deep roots in the mind of the people: the writer is someone lonely, grumpy, and poor. The question is, Why is this image so appealing?

Like so many literary creations that begin as strokes of genius and end up as tiresome clichés (Macbeth complaining about the sound and the fury, Don Quixote tilting at windmills) the image of the garret-bound writer was a mere literary creation, born, no doubt, to describe a certain writer at a certain moment, in a long-lost novel or poem. Only later did it become frozen into the commonplace that riddles us today. Writers may snigger or chuckle at this image, but the public (that vast imaginary creation) looks upon it as the truth and feels allowed to make a number of assumptions. For instance, that writers are misanthropic, that writers are creative only in the most uncomfortable conditions, that writers enjoy squalor. And, most important, that poverty is somehow part of a writer's essence. The fact that a book was written "in a bed in a garret" or that it was "begun, continued, and ended, under a long course of physic, and a great want of money," as Jonathan Swift declared in his preface to *A Tale of a Tub*, does not say much about the excellence of the book itself.

There are writers who themselves become convinced of the truth of this image and accept the role of the poor outsider without question. There is something masochistically gratifying in struggling through life for the sake of one's art, something that appeals to the Puritan dictum of suffering for the sake of glory. (The Greeks saw art and commerce as incompatible: none of the nine Muses have commercial dealings, and monetary transactions in Olympus are left in the hands of Hermes the Trickster—god of exchanges and thieves—who is the messenger of the other divinities. Like Victorian gentlemen and ladies, the Greek gods won't debase themselves by dealing directly with tradesmen.)

Being sick, being downcast, being poor doesn't suit the creative genius; it only suits the idea that the rich patron likes to have of the artist to justify tightfistedness. There is an anecdote about the film mogul Sam Goldwyn trying to buy the rights of one of Shaw's plays. Goldwyn being Goldwyn kept haggling about the price, and in the end Shaw declined to sell. Goldwyn couldn't understand why. "The trouble is, Mr. Goldwyn," Shaw said, "that you are interested only in art—and I am interested only in money."

I SHOULD HAVE LEARNED FROM MY READING THAT such misfortunes have to happen. I don't mean crass obstacles—that Odysseus's travels might be cut short by immigration officials or that Jack Hawkins might have to hand over his treasure to tax inspectors. But even the tornado that sets Dorothy on her quest, or the sardonic Cheshire Cat who explains to Alice that everyone, herself included, is mad, were for me uncomfortable catastrophes, however necessary. I wanted things to remain peacefully unchanged and for injustice not to be allowed to cross the threshold, as I knew it would. I'm superstitious: to ward off evil alterations, I tied pieces of red thread to all the doorknobs in the house.

I remember that one morning, shortly after having

reached the decisions with my partner to sell the house and pack the library, I woke up from troubled dreams and found myself thinking about Kafka. In my library, I had three shelves dedicated to Kafka, including a number of editions of *The Metamorphosis*. A question was ringing in my head: Why does Gregor Samsa's metamorphosis occur? Why is it that Gregor wakes up one morning from troubled dreams and finds himself transformed into a giant insect?

I no longer have Kafka's books at hand, but in a notebook I carry around I jotted down certain lines from his correspondence, such as this one: "We read to ask questions." Indeed. Reading Kafka, I sense that the elicited questions are always just beyond my understanding. They promise an answer but not now, perhaps next time, next page. Something in his writing—something unfinished but very precisely honed, "Etwas Gelehrtes," something carefully constructed and yet left open to the elements—allows me approximations, intuitions, half-dreams, but never total comprehension. Kafka's texts are meticulous, ironically severe, each page obtained—as he said—"through anger, blow after blow." Kafka offers me absolute uncertainties which fit so many of my own. For instance, his description of tree trunks in the snow. "Apparently they are there, lustrous, as if a small push would suffice to send them rolling. No, we can't do it, because they are firmly rooted to the ground. But see, this too is only an appearance."

Whenever I would open one of Kafka's books, it seemed as if I were granted a kind of theological intuition, a slow and gradual ascent towards a terrible god who offers us at the same time happiness and the impossibility of enjoying it. For Kafka, the Garden of Eden still exists, even if we no longer inhabit it. Like the Law outside whose doors waits the protagonist of the fable told by the priest in *The Trial*, our inaccessible Eden remains open for us until the moment of our death. Vladimir Nabokov, subtle reader of Kafka's *Metamorphosis*, recognized in the fantastic tale a description of our daily fate. "The insect into which Gregor is transformed," Nabokov told his students at the university, "is a type of cockroach that has wings below its shell. And if Gregor found these wings, he would have been able to spread them and fly out of his prison." And Nabokov added: "Like Gregor, many Johns and many Janes are not aware that they have wings under their shells, and can fly."

A year before his death, in the German spa of Müritz, Kafka met his sister Elli and her three small children. One of the children tripped and fell. The others were about to burst out laughing when Kafka, to prevent the child from feeling humiliated for his clumsiness, said to him in an admiring tone: "How well you performed that fall! And how admirably you stood up!" Perhaps we can hope (probably in vain) that Someone might one day say to us these redemptory words.

Fourth Digression

Acts of injustice which render me powerless make me feel less akin to Job than to Lear. I want to blurt out like the very foolish fond old man: "I will have such revenges on you both, / That all the world shall . . . I will do such things . . . / What they are, yet I know not: but they shall be / The terrors of the earth." "Such things" appear on my ongoing list of "Stuff to Do," unspecified but ever present, waiting for inspiration to fulfill them. I find that vengeful dreams, however imprecise and wishful, have something comforting about them, and both the dreams and the comfort can endure. I know it's a waste of emotional energy, but I hold grudges for quite a long time. Cynthia Ozick once told me that when a Jew tries out a new fountain pen, he doesn't write out his name as most people do, but the word "Amalekites," the ancient enemies of Israel, and then crosses it out, thus effecting a scriptural revenge on the tribe his people defeated so many centuries ago. Apparently the hatred still rankles, long after the last Amalekite went down to his dusty forefathers.

Hatred among the Jews may be long-lasting, but asking and offering pardon is also an old Jewish custom. On the eve of Yom Kippur, my grandmother used to follow the ritual of asking forgiveness from her relatives and friends, who in turn asked forgiveness from her. Neither was ever denied. She believed, however, that the ritual was nothing more than a formality, and used to tell of a cousin of hers who, after asking a longtime rival to forgive her, received the conciliatory response: "I wish you everything you wish me." To which the cousin replied, "So, Clara, you're starting again already?"

In spite of the soothing ritual, I have always felt the act of pardoning dangerously close to supercilious arrogance, the offended disdainfully waving away the malice enacted towards them, as if they were above all insulting attempts. However, there is perhaps an intermediate response to injury that is neither consumed with hatred nor frozen into unconditional forgiveness, a response that recognizes the nature of malicious or stupid acts of evil, but doesn't allow the attendant hurt to be everlasting. Imagining retaliation is essentially making up stories, a gratifying and healthy exercise. In such imaginings, some form of justice can be seen to be done, and satisfaction comes from the intellectual awareness of the need, not of revenge, but of not allowing evil to go unnamed. Pardon, as we know, doesn't necessarily mean absolution or amnesty, or the erasing of the offensive action from our memory. It simply means releasing the offended person from the obligation of nurturing the offense in the mind. This is what Jane Eyre does when she grants forgiveness to her evil guardian Mrs Reed. Without her pardon the chapter can't end and a new chapter begin.

Shakespeare was a keen explorer of this paradoxical quality. Almost all his plays have at least one vengeful streak in them. In *Othello*, vengeance requires a kind of eternity to quench the Moor's thirst for revenge on the maligned Cassio: "O, that the slave had forty thousand lives!" Othello cries. "One is too poor, too weak for my revenge." Dreaming of revenge, the injured person intuits that even the fulfillment of the act will not end the need for retribution. In *The Merchant of Venice*, Shylock lists this urge among the common traits of all humankind. "If you wrong us," he asks the Christian friends of Antonio, "shall we not / revenge? If we are like you in the rest, we will / resemble you in that. If a Jew wrong a Christian, / what is his humility? Revenge. If a Christian / wrong a Jew, what should his sufferance be by / Christian example? Why, revenge." In that most bloody of plays *Titus Andronicus*, Titus affirms both the irrepressible nature of revenge and also something akin to curiosity about the way in which fate will carry out this impulse. Aaron, the evil lover, describes how the passion for revenge physically possesses his whole body: "Vengeance is in my heart, death in my hand, / Blood and revenge are hammering in my head." For Marcus Andronicus, Titus's reasonable brother, revenge lies in the course of events, outside human will, in "what God will have discover'd for revenge." And in *Cymbeline,* the jealous Leonatus at the end of the play haughtily trades his right to revenge for scornful pardon: "Kneel not to me," he says to the perfidious Iachimo. "The power that I have on you is, to spare you; / The malice towards you to forgive you: live, / And deal with others better."

Maybe one day I will achieve this generously disdainful quality of forgiveness. In the meantime, a certain obstinate mournfulness overcomes me when I think of my abandoned books.

The DAY I LEFT MY LIBRARY IN FRANCE FOR THE LAST TIME, I felt desperately unhappy, and waves of remembered lines about revenge and rage and despair came "hammering in my head" as if the library were opening its books to me in a final friendly gesture. A quote from *Through the Looking-Glass* came to my rescue. To console Alice, who is feeling miserable in the alien chessboard kingdom, the White Queen instructs her, "Consider what a great girl you are. Consider what a long way you've come to-day. Consider what o'clock it is. Consider anything, only don't cry." I considered many things: the peaceful place in which the library stood, the time it had taken to build it, the books I acquired when I was there. I asked myself, What were the circumstances that led me to set up the collection about to be stashed away in numbered boxes? What quirk made me cluster these volumes into something like the colored countries on my globe? What brought on these associations that seemed to owe their meaning to faded emotions and a logic whose rules I can now no longer remember? And does my present self reflect that distant haunting? Because if every library is autobiographical, its packing up seems to have something of a self-obituary. Perhaps these questions are the true subject of this elegy.

There are certain readers for whom books exist in the moment of reading them, and later as memories of the read pages, but who feel that the physical incarnations of books are dispensable. Borges, for instance, was one of these. Those who never visited Borges's modest flat imagined his library to be as vast as that of Babel. In fact, Borges kept only a few hundred books, and even these he used to give away as gifts to visitors. Occasionally, a certain volume had sentimental or superstitious value for him, but by and large what mattered to him were a few recalled lines, not the material object in which he had found them. For me, it has always been otherwise.

Coventry Patmore, in a poem I learned by heart as a child, says that after having struck his young son for disobeying him, he went that night into the boy's bedroom and saw that

> on a table drawn beside his head,
> He had put, within his reach,

A box of counters and a red-vein'd stone,
A piece of glass abraded by the beach
And six or seven shells,
A bottle with bluebells
And two French copper coins, ranged there with
   careful art,
To comfort his sad heart.

Comfort is of the essence. The comforting objects on my own night table are (have always been) books, and my library was itself a place of comfort and quiet reassurance. It may be that books have this reassuring quality because we don't really possess them: books possess us. Julio Cortázar, warning against accepting the gift of a watch, tells his readers: "When they give you a watch, they give you the fear of losing it, of having it stolen, of letting it drop on the floor and breaking. They give you its brand and the assurance that it's a better brand than other brands, they give you the need to compare your watch with other watches. They don't give you a watch as a gift, it is you who are the gift, it is you who are being given for the birthday of the watch." Something of the sort can be said about my books.

Perhaps the books we choose determine our perdition or salvation in the eyes of whimsical gods. In her "Report on Heaven and Hell," Silvina Ocampo concluded: "The laws of heaven and hell are versatile. Whether you go to one place or the other depends on a tiny detail. I know people who, because of a broken key or a wicker cage have gone to hell, and others who because of a newspaper page or a cup of milk, to heaven." My salvation might depend on having read a certain book by Richard Outram, by William Saroyan, by Jan Morris, by Olga Sedakova.

The books in my library promised me comfort, and also the possibility of enlightening conversations. They granted me, every time I took one in my hands, the memory of friendships that required no introductions, no conventional politeness, no pretense or concealed emotion. I knew, in that familiar space between the covers, that one evening I'd pull down a volume of Dr. Johnson or Voltaire I had never opened, and I would discover a line that had been waiting for me for centuries. I was certain, without having to retrace my way through it, that Chesterton's *The Man Who Was Thursday* or a volume of Cesare Pavese's poems would be exactly what I required to put into words what I was feeling on any given morning. Books have always spoken for me, and have taught me many things long before these things came materially into my life, and the physical volumes have been for me something very much like breathing creatures that share my bed and board. This intimacy, this trust, began early on among readers.

My library, however newly built, was in essence an ancient place: its books are the earliest protagonists of our literature. The *Epic of Gilgamesh* begins not with the adventurous king but with a box at the top of a tower that contains the lapis-lazuli book in which the poem is written, and in the first pages of the *Mahabharata* the bard Ugrashravas speaks of the volumes of the sacred Vedas and of the tales in the *Bharata* that will enlighten his listeners. In early copies of the Egyptian *Book of the Dead*, the souls are seen carrying that same book on their journey to the Otherworld, one of the first *mise en abymes* in history. From those distant days on, books have defined the characters who read them or possess them, the book in the book becoming a mirror of the protagonist who is a mirror of the reader, like the play within the play that Hamlet sets up to trap his murderous uncle, and that also, implicitly, depicts the Prince himself.

The most famous and dearest of these readers (for me at least) is Alonso Quijano, the old man who becomes Don Quixote through his reading. The village priest and the barber, to cure him of what they perceive as madness, throw most of the old man's books into the fire and imprison the survivors behind a brick wall to make it appear as if the library had never existed. When after two days of convalescing, Don Quixote leaves his bed and goes to seek the comfort of his books, he doesn't find them. He is told that a wizard arrived one night on a cloud and made the books and the room they were in vanish in a puff of smoke. Cervantes doesn't tell us what Alonso Quijano feels when he hears this; he simply says that the old man remained for a full fortnight at home, without speaking a word about pursuing his knightly quest. Without his library, Alonso Quijano is no longer who he was. But then, in conversation with the barber and the priest, and remembering the books that had taught him of the world's need for the ethics of chivalry, his imaginative strength comes back to him. He leaves his house, recruits a neighboring peasant, Sancho Panza, as his squire, and sets off on new adventures in which, though he will continue to see the world through the printed word of stories, he no longer requires them in a material sense. Having lost his books as objects, Don Quixote rebuilds his library in his mind and finds in the remembered pages the source for renewed strength. For the rest of the novel Don Quixote will no longer read a book, any book, even that which tells of his own adventures when he and Sancho discover their chronicle in print in a press of Barcelona, or those the innkeeper shows him, because now Don Quixote has attained the state of perfect readership, knowing his books by heart in the strictest sense of the word.

I've read *Don Quixote* many times since my high school days, and I've always felt, especially in the chapter in which Quijano discovers his loss, a deep sympathy for the deceived old man. Now, having lost my own library, I think I can better understand what he went through and why he set off once again into the world. Loss helps you remember, and loss of a library helps you remember who you truly are.

Fifth Digression

Perhaps the greatest loss of a library (but the loss of any library is incommensurable) took place on a day that our histories mysteriously have not recorded. We don't know exactly when the library that came to stand as the model for all libraries, the Library of Alexandria, came to an end. In fact, we know nothing, or almost nothing, of the great library except its fame. Kingsley's description is probably closer to an Alma-Tadema painting of his own time than to the library contemporary travelers thought too well known to bother describing. We don't have a single account of how it functioned, what it looked like, how big it was, who were the readers who studied there. We can surmise some of these things from different sources, but all we have are stories (probably true) about its creation and stories (probably false) about its end.

The Library of Alexandria, as far as we can tell, was founded in the third century B.C.E. by Ptolemy I, a Macedonian general who had served under Alexander the Great, who in turn had been tutored by Aristotle. Legend has it that the library was built around the core of books left by Aristotle to one of his students, Demetrius of Phaleron, and housed in the Mouseion, the house of the Muses, daughters of the goddess Memory. To feed the voracious enterprise, the Ptolemaic kings ordered that every book in their realm be bought or copied and transported to the library, which, at the height of its fame, is said to have held close to half a million scrolls. Ships sailing into Alexandria were searched for books they might be carrying. If any were found, they were confiscated by the port authorities, copied, and then returned, though at times the copies, not the originals, were given back to their owners.

For at least three centuries, the Library of Alexandria held under its roof most of the Mediterranean world's memory. Its end came under circumstances as uncertain as those of its existence. Writing almost a century after the surmised events, Plutarch tells us that the library was consumed in a fire started by Julius Caesar's troops in 48 B.C.E. during the siege of Alexandria, a story that today appears doubtful to most scholars, who believe that the fire destroyed only the stores near the port, which held the overflow of books. Perhaps the appeal of this account, many times repeated, is the schadenfreude of knowing that the presumptuous library met its end in a fire as fierce as its ambition.

Whatever the cause, after the destruction, readers in Alexandria used a "daughter library" housed in the Serapeum, a temple erected in another part of the city, and this too was accorded a tragic end. According to the fifth-century historian Socrates of Constantinople, in 391 the Coptic pope Theophilus ordered that the Serapeum be torn down. It was a time of endings. That same year, Emperor Theodosius I banned pagan rituals and decreed Christianity as the state religion, closed all non-Christian schools of philosophy, banned all pagan places of worship, and extinguished the sacred fire in the Temple of Vesta in Rome.

One of the first scholars to work in the library was Callimachus, a Greek poet and critic. He was wonderfully prolific. The tenth-century Byzantine encyclopedia known as the Suda credits him with over 800 books of which only 6 hymns and 64 epigrams survive. His punctilious erudition earned him a reputation for elitism and pedantry. Devoted to the library and its ambition, Callimachus compiled a 120-volume catalogue of "All Those Books Preeminent in Literature." The Pinakes, as the catalogue was known, became a sort of annotated canon of the most important writings (according to Callimachus's learned opinion) in the almost incommensurable collection. The Pinakes is now lost to us, as are most of the books and authors it was supposed to make live forever.

Callimachus believed that reading grants books and their authors life throughout eternity. In a poem dedicated to Heraclitus, he makes this thought explicit:

Long ago you turned to ashes, my Halicarnassian
    friend,
but your poems, your nightingales, live on.
Hades clutches all things yet can't touch these.

Perhaps. A few books survive the destruction of a library, and a few authors cling to the raft of their surviving books. But others come to their end with the edifice that contained them. My Latin teacher would say, "We must be grateful that we don't know what the great books were that perished in Alexandria, because if we knew what they were, we'd be inconsolable."

We know, however, of a handful. Almost certainly among those lost was Homer's comic epic the *Margites*, which for Aristotle was the predecessor of all comedies, "as the *Iliad* and the *Odyssey* are of our tragedies." The second book of Aristotle's *Poetics* (which provides a motive for the murderer in Umberto Eco's *The Name of the Rose*) disappeared in the library's wake. Also gone are most of the works by the major Greek dramatists. According to ancient sources, the library held 90 plays by Euripides, 70 (some say 90) by Aeschylus, and 123 by Sophocles. Of this vast collection, other than scattered fragments, only 18 plays by Euripides, 7 by Aeschylus, and 7 by Sophocles have come down to us in their entirety.

Callimachus died in 240 B.C.E., the year when another librarian of Alexandria, Eratosthenes, who was said to have founded the science of geography, calculated the circumference of the earth with a 2 percent error. During his time as chief librarian, Eratosthenes succeeded in obtaining for the library the official Athenian copies (the closest thing to the originals) of the works of the three greatest Greek dramatists: Sophocles, Aeschylus, and Euripides. He managed to have the king of Alexandria agree to pledge the equivalent in today's currency of four million dollars as a guarantee against the precious manuscripts. However, once the scrolls arrived in Alexandria, Eratosthenes had the king forfeit the deposit, made copies of the manuscripts, and returned the copies to Athens. The Athenians, having both the texts and the money, were deemed satisfied.

Sometimes miracles occur. A few years ago, a young French scholar rooting about in the National Library of Athens found what he thought was (and that proved to be) a long-lost letter by Galen, the second-century Greek physician. Galen had collected a valuable library of medical manuscripts, and also works by Aristotle, Plato, and others, which he had carefully annotated in his own hand. Because the collection seemed to him too precious to leave unguarded in his house in Rome, Galen placed it in a storehouse near the port of Ostia, judged extremely secure because government guards were posted at its gate to ensure the safety of the grain silos. However, a fire broke out one night, reducing to ashes both the grain and Galen's books. A friend wrote to Galen commiserating on his loss, and the physician answered him in a letter (unearthed by the French scholar) in which he stoically refuses to mourn his vanished library and instead tells his friend, in great detail, about his burnt books and how he had read and annotated them.

"Collecting: to assert control over what's unbearable," says Ruth Padel. I think this has always been the unrealized wish in my relationship to books. Present, as solid objects, we imagine books to be inert and passive, and so devoid of intellect that we allow ourselves to invest them with meanings of our own making. To the Samarian question "Can these stones live?" we answer "Yes" and proceed to make books into familiars, transforming them into the presences among which we dwell. In my library, I felt surrounded by this "silent majority" (as Homer called the dead), a vast flock of pages that held the keys to my past and instructions for my present, and also useful charms for my daily rituals. All these, except for their vaguely remembered shadows, are now lost, at least for the time being.

Maybe loss is an inherited trait. My maternal grandmother had a gift for losing things. She had emigrated
as a teenager from the outskirts of Ekaterinburg to one
of Baron Hirsch's colonies in the Argentinean Mesopotamia, and from that world of Jewish gauchos to the Jewish
neighborhood of Buenos Aires, known as the Once. Even
within the confines of her small apartment, she managed
to lose things. Her lace-lined handkerchief would mysteriously disappear somewhere in the abysmal depths of
her black handbag. The matches she needed to light the
Shabbat candles would vanish from their allotted place
next to the samovar. When she needed ground cinnamon
for her quince strudel, the white pepper would appear
like a ghost in its place, and when she needed the pepper
for her gefilte fish the space for the pepper in her spice
rack would be empty. My grandmother lost receipts, pho-
tographs, stockings, documents, jewelry, money. She lost
her tram ticket so often that the inspectors (who recognized her after decades of seeing her on the same tram
along the same route) would simply pass her by with
a nod and a smile. My mother would buy her support
stockings by the dozen, and she kept my grandmother's
identity card in the safe in our house. And yet, losing
things didn't worry my grandmother. "We lost our house
in Russia, we lost our friends, we lost our parents. I lost
my husband. I lost my language," she'd say in a curious
mixture of Russian, Yiddish, and Spanish. "Losing things

is not so bad because you learn to enjoy not what you have but what you remember. You should grow accustomed to loss."

I think this is true. There exists, perhaps, in all human imagination, an unspoken expectation of losing what has been achieved. You build, of course, because you want a family, a house, a business. If you can, you create something out of sounds and colors and words. You compose a song, you paint a picture, you write a book. But underlying all you do is the secret knowledge that everything will one day be swept away: the song will no longer be sung, the picture will fade, the book will go up in flames until the day yet to come (as Isaiah says) when we shall be given beauty for ashes.

But to lose one must first find. If loss (or its possibility) is inherent in every intent, in every hope, then that intent, that hope, that desire to build something that comes to life from the ashes is correspondingly a part of everything we lose. Even though history has taught us that nothing lasts for long, the impulse to create in the face of impending destruction, to resettle in foreign lands and reproduce ancestral models, to build new libraries is a powerful and unquenchable impulse.

For all three Peoples of the Book, for the three antagonistic children of Abraham, the Word and the World are powerfully intertwined. The first verse of the Gospel of John, "In the beginning was the Word," applies to all three cultures. God, the plural Elohim of the Jews who is One and Alone; the divine Trinity of Christians who is both One and Three; the singular Allah of Muslims who speaks through his Prophet—all create through the word. The world, according to these three faiths, is the breath or enunciation of God, who, further to his creation, annotates or comments on his spoken text in writing: in the Laws given to Moses, in the words of Christ transcribed by the apostles, in the Qur'an revealed to Muhammad. (In this last instance, no single word can be translated or changed even by one letter since for Muslims the Qur'an is one of the attributes of God himself, like his omnipresence and omnipotence.)

Our languages, according to the biblical legend, are God's gift (or punishment) bestowed after Babel, when God shattered the single tongue spoken by all humankind into the myriad tongues we speak today. Therefore, since language comes from God, God reveals himself in every word we use, and hides himself in every statement. In 1890, in the old Jewish neighborhood in Cairo, in the sealed storage room of a medieval synagogue, one of the largest and most precious ancient archives in existence was discovered, in which papers of all sorts had been amassed (official documents, poems, shopping lists, letters, treatises, and so on) because it was believed that no piece of writing should be thrown away or destroyed, since it might contain, unawares, the name of God. God-given language implies both the freedom and restriction to name, and the prohibition against destroying the unnamable.

Every time we put something into words, we simultaneously pronounce a declaration of faith in the power of language to re-create and communicate our experience of the world, and our admission of its shortcomings to name this experience fully. Faith in language is, like all true faiths, unaltered by everyday practice that contradicts its claims of power—unaltered in spite of our knowledge that whenever we try to say something, however simple, however clear-cut, only a shadow of that something travels from our conception to its utterance, and further from its utterance to its reception and understanding. Every time we say "Pass the salt," we do indeed convey, in essence, our request; and, in essence, our request is understood. But the shades and echoes of meaning, the private connotations and cultural roots, personal, social, and symbolic, emotional and objective, cannot, each and every one of them, travel with our words, so those who hear or read us must reconstruct, as best they can, around the core or under the shell of those words, the universe of sense and emotion and meaning in which they were born. Plato, who would have agreed with my grandmother that everything is subject to loss, believed that our experience of the world consisted of nothing but intimations of meaning and shadows on the wall of a cave. If that is so, what we put into words are the shadows of shadows, and every book confesses the impossibility of holding fully onto whatever it is that our experience seizes. All our libraries are the glorious record of that failure.

Sixth Digression

But there is more. Not only did God, according to Scripture, limit the power of our words: our other powers of creation were also censored. The Second Commandment of the Decalogue reads, "Thou shalt not make unto thee any graven image, or any likeness of any thing that is in the heaven above, or that is in the earth beneath, or that is in the water under the earth." Though the commandment carries on to say that "thou shalt not bow down thyself to them, nor serve them: for I the Lord thy God am a jealous God," it is the first part of the prohibition that long presented a problem for believers. Did God forbid only the creation of graven images of worship, or did his commandment extend to the creation of any image, any representation, any art by any means whatsoever, stone or color or words? Psalm 97 glosses this commandment: "Confounded be all they that serve graven images, that boast themselves of idols." In the eighteenth century, the celebrated Hassidic master Rabbi Nahman of Bratslav explained the prohibition as follows: "The idol is destined to come and spit in the face of those who worship it and put them to shame, then bow before the Holy One, blessed be He, and cease to exist." Rabbi Nahman did not pronounce himself specifically on the acts of sculpting, painting, and fiction writing, but a condemnation of these crafts is implicit in his prophecy.

Rabbinical commentators, and of course artists and writers, have pondered the question ever since. To a certain extent, from a biblical perspective, the history of the human imagination can be seen as the history of the debate on this peculiar interdiction. Is creation a permissible endeavor within the human scope, or are we condemned to fail because all art, since it is human and not divine, carries within it its own failure? God says he is a jealous God: Is he also a jealous artist? According to a Talmudic commentary quoted by Louis Ginzberg in *Legends of the Jews*, the serpent said to Eve in the Garden: "God Himself ate first of the fruit of the tree, and then He created the world. Therefore doth He forbid you to eat thereof, lest you create other worlds. Because everyone knows that 'artisans of the same guild hate one another.'" It is tempting for artists and writers to believe that they are in the same guild as the one who created them and granted them their creative powers.

One of the most explicit versions of this paradox is illustrated in the legend of the Golem, which I believe can serve as a metaphor for the library. *Golem* is a word that first appears in Psalm 139: "Thine eyes did see my *golem*." According to Rabbi Eliezer, writing in the first century C.E., the word *golem* means "an unarticulated lump." The eighteenth-century legend of the Golem, this "unarticulated lump," tells of how the Maharal of Prague (an acronym for Morenu Harav Rabbi Laib, "our teacher Rabbi Loew") created a creature out of clay to protect the Jews from pogroms. On the forehead of the creature, Rabbi Loew wrote the word *emet*, "truth," and this enabled the creature to come to life and assist the rabbi in his daily chores. Later, however, the Golem escaped his master's control and wrought havoc in the ghetto, and Rabbi Loew was obliged to return it to the dust by effacing the first letter of *emet*, so that the word now read *met*, "death."

The Golem has prestigious ancestors. In a Talmudic passage of the Sanhedrin, it is stated that in the fourth century C.E., the Babylonian teacher Rava created a man out of clay and sent it to Rabbi Zera, who tried to converse with it, and when he saw that the creature could not utter a single word, he said to it, "You belong to the spawn of wizards; return to the dust." Immediately the creature crumbled into a shapeless heap. Another passage explains that in the third century, two Palestinian masters, Rabbi Haninah and Rabbi Oshea, with the help of the *Sefer Yetzirah*, or Book of Creation, brought to life a calf every Sabbath eve, which they then cooked for dinner.

Inspired by the eighteenth-century legend of Rabbi Loew, in 1915 the Austrian writer Gustav Meyrink published *The Golem*, a fantastic novel about a creature who appears every thirty-three years at the unreachable window of a circular room without doors in the Prague ghetto. Meyrink's novel was to have an unexpected offspring. That same year, the sixteen-year-old Jorge Luis Borges, trapped with his family in Switzerland during the war, read Meyrink's *Golem* in German and was enthralled by its haunting atmosphere. "Everything in the book is uncanny," he would later write, "even the monosyllables of the table of contents: Prag, Punsch, Nacht, Spuk, Licht . . ." Borges saw in Meyrink's *Golem* "a fiction made up of dreams that enclose other dreams," and allowed its fantastic vision of the world to lay the foundations for much of his future fiction.

More than forty years later, in 1957, Borges included the Golem in an early version of his *Book of Imaginary Beings*; a year later he told the story of Rabbi Loew in what was to become one of his most famous poems, first published in the Buenos Aires magazine *Davar* in the winter of 1958. Afterwards, Borges included the Golem poem in his *Personal Anthology*, placing it before a short text titled "*Inferno*, I:32," which considers, from different perspectives, the same existential question concerning the limits of creation. In the poem, Rabbi Loew wonders why he was driven to fashion this "apprentice of man" and what might be the meaning of his creature; in the text on Dante's *Inferno*, the panther that appears at the beginning of the poem and then the dying poet himself both learn and afterwards forget why it is that they have been created. Borges's "Golem" ends with this quatrain:

> In the hour of anguish and dim light
> The rabbi looked in awe upon his Golem.
> Who will tell us what was felt by God
> Looking upon his own rabbi in Prague?

The theme of the Golem haunted Borges for many years. When he visited Israel in 1969, he asked to meet the famous scholar of Jewish mysticism Gershom Scholem, whose name he had used in the poem "as the only possible word to rhyme with 'Golem' in Spanish." Their conversation, I was told, centered on the Jewish notion of permissible creation. Like the ancient biblical commentators, Borges and Scholem debated the fundamental question: To what success can an artist aspire? How can a writer achieve his purpose when all he has at his disposal is the imperfect tool of language? And above all: What is created when an artist sets out to create? Does a new, forbidden world come into being or is a dark mirror of this world lifted up for us to gaze in? Is a work of art a lasting reality or an imperfect lie?

Is it a living Golem or a dead handful of dust? How can the Jews accept that at the same time God has granted them both the gift of creation and the prohibition to use it? And finally, even if there were an answer to these questions, can we know it? Scholem reminded Borges of Kafka's unappealable dictum: "If it had been possible to build the Tower of Babel without climbing it, it would have been allowed."

Jorge Luis Borges died in Geneva at 7:47 a.m., on 14 June 1986. As a special favor, the Administrative Council of Geneva decided to grant him permission to be buried in the cemetery of Plainpalais, reserved for the great and famous Swiss, since Borges had often spoken of Geneva as "my other homeland." In memory of Borges's grandmothers, one Catholic and the other Protestant, the service was read by Father Pierre Jacquet and Pastor Edouard de Montmollin. Pastor Montmollin's address judiciously opened with the first verse of the Gospel of John. "Borges," said Pastor Montmollin, "was a man who unceasingly searched for the right word, the term that would sum up the whole, the final meaning of things," and went on to explain that, as the Good Book taught us, a man can never reach that word by his own efforts. As John made clear, it is not we who discover the Word, but the Word that reaches us. Pastor Montmollin summed up precisely Borges's literary credo: the writer's task is to find the right words to name the world, knowing all the while that these words are, as words, unreachable. Words are our only tools both to lend and to recover meaning and, at the same time, they allow us to understand that meaning, they show us that it lies precisely beyond the pale of words, just on the other side of language. Translators, perhaps more than any other wordsmiths, know this: whatever we build out of words can never seize in its entirety the desired object. The Word that is in the beginning names but can never be named.

Throughout his life, Borges explored and tried out this truth. From his first readings in Buenos Aires to the final writings dictated on his deathbed in Geneva, every text became, in his mind, proof of the literary paradox of being named without quite naming anything into being. Ever since his adolescence, something in every book he read seemed to escape him, like a wayward monster, promising, however, a further page, a greater epiphany at the next reading. And something in every page he wrote forced him to confess that the author was not the ultimate master of his own creation, of his Golem. This double bind, the promise of revelation that every book grants its reader and the warning of defeat that every book gives its writer, lends the literary act its constant fluidity.

For Borges, this fluidity lends both richness and an element of tragedy to Dante's *Commedia*. According to Borges, Dante attempted to create a universe of words in which the poet is absolute master: a world in which he can enjoy the love of his adored Beatrice, converse with his beloved Virgil, renew friendships with absent friends, reward with a place in heaven those he deems worthy of reward, and take revenge on his enemies by condemning them to hell. The ancient dictum "Nomina sunt consequentia rerum," "words are the fruit of things," can work both ways, as the Kabbalists taught, basing their belief on the Adam story in Genesis. If words exist because they correspond to existing things, then things might exist because there are words to name them.

And yet, in literature, things do not work out that way. Literature follows rules that override the rules of words and the rules of reality. "Each literary work entrusts to its writer the form that it is seeking," Borges wrote in the preface to his last book, *Los conjurados*. "Entrusts," he wrote; he could have written "commands." He could also have added that no writer, not even Dante, can fully accomplish the command.

For Borges, the *Commedia*, the most perfect of human literary endeavors, was nevertheless a failed creation because it failed to become what the author intended. The Word that breathes life (both Borges and Dante realized) is not equivalent to the living creature who breathes the word: the word that remains on the page, the word that, while imitating life, is incapable of being life. Plato made Socrates decry the creations of artists and poets for that very reason: art is imitation, never the real thing. If success were possible (it is not) the universe would become redundant. The most to which we can aspire is an inexpressible epiphany, like the one that rewards Dante at the end of his journey, at which "high fantasy loses its power" and will and desire turn over like a perfect wheel, moved by love.

Whether because of the imperfection of our tools or the imperfection of ourselves, whether because of the jealousy of the Godhead or his concern with our indulging in redundant tasks, the ancient prohibition of the Decalogue continues to serve as warning and incitement. The dusty and unsatisfactory Golem that still haunts our dreams through the dark alleyways of Prague is, after all, the uttermost achievement to which our crafts can aspire: bringing the dust to life and having it do our bidding. When the Weizmann Institute in Rehovot, Israel, built its first computer, Gershom Scholem suggested that it be named Golem I.

Our creations, our Golems or our libraries, are at best things that suggest an approximation to a copy of our blurry intuition of the real thing, itself an imperfect imitation of an ineffable archetype. This achievement is our unique and humble prerogative. The only art that is synonymous with reality is (according to Dante and Borges and the Talmudic scholars) that of God. Gazing upon the pathway to Eden, sculpted by God himself in the Purgatory of the Proud, Dante says that "he saw not better than I saw, who saw the scenes in real life." God's reality and God's representation of reality are identical. Ours are not.

So it is that writers are made to play the role of a poor Golem, imperfectly created and capable only of imperfection, incompetent creatures casting in turn blasphemous doubts on the perfection of their Maker. In this game of shifting mirrors, the faulty Golem becomes our modest, faulty, all-embracing literature, and literature becomes the Golem. Yes, but an immortal Golem, because even when the first letter of the writing on its forehead is effaced, and *emet* becomes *met*, a word still stands to name for us yet another unnamable: death itself, the end of all creation.

Jews believe that humans are made of time, that a ritual continuity flows through their veins reaching back to the drawn-out time of Abraham. Perhaps it is for that reason that for Jews loss is not of the essence: the rhythm of life continues in spite of the disappearance of material things. Jews, after all, are a nomad people, for whom leaving things behind is an everyday experience, for whom exile is a condition of being and settlement only a halt on the flight from Egypt. Jews, like Moses, are always within sight of the Promised Land but never there, even after they have reached Zion—because even though God promised Moses a land destined for him, that land must remain forever unreachable, like Kafka's Castle. The curse of the Wandering Jew who can never rest until the Christian Second Coming is merely the confirmation of a natural state of being among Jews: the Jew must wait for the Second Coming because, in the Jew's heart, the First Coming has not yet taken place. And given the nature of the world, it will not take place any time soon.

This is the paradox of all our arts and crafts: to exist between these two mandates, like ambitious but imperfectly gifted Kabbalists. Jews live in the grip of an immemorial and contradictory injunction: on one hand, not to build things that might lead to idolatry and complacency; on the other, to build things worthy of adoration—to reject the serpent's temptation to aspire to be gods and also to reflect God's creation back to him in luminous pages that conjure up his world; to accept that the limits of human creation are hopelessly unlike the limitless creation of God, and yet to strive continuously to attain those limits to set up something that aspires to an order, a imperfect dream of order, a library.

THIS SENSE OF LIVING WITHIN THE MODEL OF THAT which we attempt to reproduce in words and images is everywhere present, taunting us, daring us to try. For example, my boxed-up books have conjured up doppelgängers in the places in which I now live. On Broadway, between 72nd and 74th Streets sidewalk vendors display piles of books on trestle tables. I stop every time I go by and glance through the paperback spines and the mostly tattered hardbacks. Often I come across titles I recognize, sometimes in the same edition I collected in my library or had in my distant adolescence (but no longer have), ghostly reminders of another place and another time. I pick up the book, I leaf through it, I read a line here and there. Is this really the same book I held in my hands faraway and long ago? Is this copy identical to the one in which I read for the first time Hesse's story of Prince Siddhartha or Margaret Mead's chronicle of adolescents in Samoa? The legend of the double says that one can recognize the other because the imposter casts no shadow. Here too, the doppelgänger of the book I held in my hands is shadowless, something without a past. Each reading experience is unique to its place and time, and cannot be duplicated. In spite of my hopes, I know that no library can be fully resurrected.

One of the most common of literary commonplaces is that the number of plots imaginable is vast but limited. Might this be true of libraries as well? The number of combinations of books, though unthinkably great, is not infinite. Lewis Carroll, over a century and a half ago, summed up this dizzying notion in *Sylvie and Bruno*. "The day must come," he wrote, "when every possible *book* will be written. For the number of *words* is finite." And he added, "Instead of saying *'what* book shall I write?' an author will ask himself *'which* book shall I write?'" We seem condemned to repetition.

But is this repetition due to the feeble capabilities of the human mind or to our associative perceptions as readers? "Since life is a voyage or a battle," remarked Raymond Queneau, "every story is either the *Iliad* or the *Odyssey*." Are we incapable of conceiving of an entirely new story or do we recognize in every story traces of our previous readings? Does the fact that *Adventures of Pinocchio* seems to me like a rewriting of *Adventures of Telemachus* (both tell the story of a boy in search of his father) and every new trashy novel like every old trashy novel depend on the scarcity of provisions in our mental pantry or on our ability to recognize the Jamesian figures in our carpets?

I suspect that there is a third possibility. We like repetition. As children we ask that the same story be read to us in exactly the same manner, again and again. As adults, though we declare a passion for novelty, we seek out the same toys to which we have grown accustomed, mostly under the appearance of different gadgets, with the same bewildering determination with which we elect the same politicians under the guise of different masks. In this, Chesterton thought we were like God, who, according to him, exults in monotony. "It is possible," wrote Chesterton, "that God says every morning, 'Do it again' to the sun; and every evening, 'Do it again' to the moon." We feel that there is comfort in sameness.

The ancients weren't troubled by originality. The stories Homer told were long familiar to his listeners, and Dante could count on his audience knowing (all too well) of the sins punished in hell and the gossip about Paolo and Francesca. The things to come were already part of our experience, even if poorly remembered or faintly recognized. History was a repetition of circles, as Giambattista Vico understood, and we ascended (or descended) through spirals of time and circles of knowledge as if revisiting old and familiar places. We dislike being surprised.

So perhaps in our new age of anxiety we seek consolation in telling the same old stories over and over again because they strengthen our hope that *plus ça change, plus ça reste tel quel.* Our childhood heroes—Superman, Batman, and other sexy musclemen—have returned to help us imagine that it is possible to fight for justice, and Sherlock Holmes has come out of his beekeeping retirement to solve hideous problems in the century of electronic villains and financial crooks. Shakespeare drew his plots from Boccaccio and Bandello; we draw ours from Hollywood films.

Is there a danger of stagnation in repetition? I don't think so. Inevitably, every time we repeat a story we add to the previous repetitions. Every story is a palimpsest, composed of layers of tellings and retellings, and every time we think we are parroting a well-known anecdote the words shed their feathers and sprout new ones for the occasion. The law of Borges's Pierre Menard, that every text becomes a different text with every new reading, applies to the whole of literature. This is perhaps the shadow side of the greedy desire to read everything, a desire Thomas De Quincey described as "absolutely endless and inexorable as the grave."

The constancy we seek in life, the repetition of stories

that seems to assure us that everything will remain as it was then and is now, is, as we know, illusory. Our fate (Ovid has been telling us this for centuries) is change, our nature is to change, and every story we tell and every story we read is like Heraclitus's river, a metaphor that (this too) we shall go on repeating. A Welsh poem from the sixth century (which I rediscovered by chance leafing through a book I remembered in one of those Broadway sidewalk offerings) celebrates this continuity of change.

I have been a multitude of shapes,
Before I assumed a consistent form.
I have been a sword, narrow, variegated,
I will believe when it is apparent.
I have been a tear in the air,
I have been the dullest of stars.
I have been a word among letters,
I have been a book.

It is trite to say that the past can't be relived, but in discoveries like these I experience something old and new at the same time. That is to say, the fingers that now turn the pages as I stand on the sidewalk among the passersby execute the same gesture they made long ago, on a morning when they were not stiff and speckled and gnarled. But now the gesture has become part of a conscious ritual, enacted every time I come across the same book with the same remembered cover, now layered with clusters of experience. One of Kafka's aphorisms reads, "Leopards break into the temple and drink from the sacrificial vessels. This keeps happening. In the end, it can be foreseen and it is incorporated into the ritual." Holding the double of a book that was once mine becomes part of my new reading rituals. I now realize that throughout my life, I've shed these rituals and found new ones over and over again.

The ritual of resurrection is perhaps more frequent than we care to admit and happens in myriad ways. Shortly before my taking the decision to dismantle and pack the library and leave France for good, the director of cultural programming of the Bibliothèque et Archives nationales du Québec, Nicole Vallières, wrote to me to say that she wanted to celebrate the tenth anniversary of the institution with an exhibition around one of my books, *The Library at Night.* I accepted with enthusiasm, but suggested that instead of displaying my printed copy and its manuscript (which would have been, in my opinion, a somewhat dreary exhibition) Vallières ask Robert Lepage to imagine a show based on the book. Lepage, one of the world's greatest theater directors, is always involved in dozens of projects, but to our delight he accepted and began to imagine an interactive creation on the theme of libraries. I had known Lepage ever since the productions of his first plays in Toronto in the mid-eighties, and had followed much of his work since, but I never expected to work with him on a project. The result (entirely Lepage's creation) opened on 27 October 2015 and was miraculous.

The public descended into one of the exhibition spaces of the library and in small groups was ushered into a room that imaginatively reproduced my lost library in France. After hearing a short meditation on the nature of libraries, the visitors were given 3-D viewing goggles and led into another, larger space planted with high birch trees, down a carpet of scattered leaves (seemingly torn from my books), to long tables at which they were invited to sit. Placing the goggles over their eyes, they saw ten different symbols that allowed them to choose one of ten famous libraries to visit: the library of Admont Abbey in Austria, the Library of Alexandria, the Library of Congress in Washington, D.C., the Royal Library of Denmark in Copenhagen, Vasconcelos Library in Mexico City, the National Library of Bosnia and Herzegovina in Sarajevo, the Parliamentary Library of Ottawa, the Sainte-Geneviève Library in Paris, the library of the Hase-dera temple in Japan, and (because imaginary libraries have their legitimate place in the world) the library that Captain Nemo set up in his *Nautilus*. The experience of visiting these libraries through the magic of the 3-D goggles was hallucinatory. You lost the sense of your body, of the floor beneath your feet, of the other visitors, and you believed you truly were in one of those venerable halls, surrounded by thousands of precious books and a few phantom readers. But for me, it was the first space that touched me most of all. After having said good-bye to the house in which I had lived for so long and packed my books, not knowing when I would see them again, I was moved by the sight of the reconstructed bookshelves, the stone walls, the small windows streaked with gusts of rain as if by the apparition of the ghost of a dear dead friend. I felt that the library I had lost had been transformed into a different one, the now shared symbol of something that I could only vaguely understand but knew to be real. The god Proteus could change his shape until someone grabbed him and held him secure: then he would allow himself to be seen as he really was, as a blending of all his metamorphoses. So it was with my library. It changed and dissolved and was set up once more, and was lost again, until the moment when its imagined self was conjured up before me. Then it ceased to be a hope, brave guesswork, a material place and became, thanks to Lepage, with astonishing conviction, an epiphany.

This experience had for me something of the experience of certain dreams. For many years now, I've had a recurrent dream. I'm in a library—faintly lit, like the one in France, by green-shaded lamps, with a high-beamed ceiling almost invisible—and I walk endlessly down the book-lined corridor imagining what the volumes are whose spines I barely distinguish. I realize that these imagined books are a dream in the dream, and I begin to reconstruct in my mind the texts that I think I have read, or want one day to read, or have read and forgotten. I remember a passage in one of Nathaniel Hawthorne's notebooks. One day in 1842, the thirty-eight-year-old Hawthorne wrote, "To write a dream, which shall resemble the real course of a dream, with all its inconsistency, its eccentricities and aimlessness—with nevertheless a leading idea running through the whole. Up to this old age of the world, no such thing has ever been written."

Seventh Digression

From the first dream of Gilgamesh four thousand years ago on to our time, Hawthorne's observation proves to be right. Something in the retelling of a dream, however haunting and however true, lacks the peculiar verisimilitude of dreams, their unique vocabulary and texture, their singular identity.

It is possible that Hawthorne, himself the writer of remarkable dreams, was pointing at something more than the ineffability of dreams, something to do with the nature of language and storytelling. As we learn to our cost, language always approximates, never seizes completely whatever it is that it wants to tell. Naming a thing or a condition, describing a place or an event, a writer uses language to build a verbal imagery out of a few chosen bits and pieces of a reality perceived or imagined to be perceived, all the while recognizing the incapability of encompassing the whole in all its fleeting dimensions. And yet, in order to engage the reader in a mutual contract of faith, the writer must pretend that the reality portrayed in words has factual precision and coherence. So ingrained is this procedure that a writer often attempts to disguise this supposed precision with rhetorical tricks: for instance, by not revealing everything ("En un lugar de la Mancha de cuyo nombre no quiero acordarme") or by pretending not to reveal everything ("Call me Ishmael").

But in the case of dreams, such devices are ineffectual. Real dreams don't assume the all-knowing confidence of waking life. Dreams don't imply, as waking life does, a provable, tangible state of being that would require only infinite time and flawless senses for us to perceive it entirely. Dreams humbly admit their imperfect condition, their kaleidoscopic, changing, fleeting nature. Hawthorne says he discerns in dreams "a leading idea running through the whole" like a narrative backbone, but in this he may be merely hopeful. Too often dreams appear in disconnected fragments, like the scattered pages from the universal book that Dante saw gathered in the final ineffable vision. Psychoanalysis teaches us that our psyche learns to read a narrative in this randomness, but then we can read narrative in anything, even in the meaningless cosmos. After all, our species is perhaps best defined as the reading animals.

But if we admit that the waking life, which we do quite successfully put into stories, also has an incoherence of its own, then the telling of dreams can be seen as simply another manner of storytelling, neither more nor less accurate than a realistic novel. Astrophysics uses mathematical formulas to discover the laws that rule the universe, common laws for all things big and small, while simultaneously admitting that the models of the universe produced by these formulas lie outside our capabilities of representation. Stephen Hawking, for example, has confessed that the theories he has developed to explain certain cosmic mysteries assume a cosmic model that he himself cannot visualize. If that is the case, if manageable mathematical formulas serve to unscramble what cannot be concretely imagined, then why not allow our capabilities of representation to build models of the world that will stand for our experience of the world, while simultaneously admitting that the world itself refuses to be pictured or named.

Alice, whose experience of dreams is one of the deepest and most convincing in all literature, is quite ready to admit that words cannot be used to name the endless plurality of the world. When Humpty Dumpty tells her that he uses the word *glory* to mean "there's a nice knock-down argument for you," Alice objects that *glory* does not mean "a nice knock-down argument." "When I use a word," says Humpty Dumpty in a rather scornful tone, "it means just what I choose it to mean—neither more nor less." "The question is," Alice objects, "whether you *can* make words mean so many different things." "The question is," Humpty Dumpty answers, "which is to be master—that's all." No doubt the writer's task is to embrace Humpty Dumpty's faith in the powers of language, and be the master, while at the same time convincing Alice that he submits to the rules of a shared understanding, rules over which the words themselves hold dominion. Of course, both Humpty Dumpty and Alice, both writer and reader, know, more or less consciously, that this is all a pretense to which we must resign ourselves if literature is to exist at all.

But in the same way that we cannot deliberately, faithfully construct a dream while asleep, awake we are unable to put into words the complexity of the universe. To avoid, or bypass, this incompetence, a literary dream, the story of a dream, must be organized differently, made to assume other objectives, appear less keen to reproduce a real dream than to fit something called "a dream" into the logic and tone of the narrative. Perhaps the only success to which the writer can aspire in dream telling is to make the reader believe that the characters themselves believe the dream to be a dream. It doesn't matter if we as readers (to use three biblical examples) know that the dreams that Joseph tells his brothers are meant to be prophetic, or that the dreams that Nebuchadnezzar tells Daniel are meant to be allegorical, or that Joseph's dream about Mary's pregnancy is meant to be explanatory: each of these dreams works within the narrative that contains it and is justified by it and illuminates it.

Sometimes the story only pretends to be a dream. We accept, but are not really convinced, that Bunyan's *Pilgrim's Progress* is the story of a dream, or that Dorothy's adventures in Oz are a dream. This method of framing the narrative in a dream is a sort of excuse for the writer, who can then argue that, since this is a dream, everything that takes place in it is possible. However, rather than add verisimilitude to the story, such devices make the reader conscious of how even the attempt at the incoherence of a dream must answer to strict laws of fictional logic. Things may happen that in a realistic story would perhaps be impossible, but even the impossible things must follow rules of cause and consequence. After running away from home, Christian can arrive in any country, and after being whisked away by the tornado, Dorothy can land anywhere in the world, but in both cases it must be somewhere, and that somewhere must be mapped for the reader's guidance. The surrealists, as we know, attempted a few deliberately incoherent dream narratives, but we read them less as examples of real dreams than as displays of verbal dexterity.

Sometimes the story tells a dream only to better question the nature of what we call reality, as in the famous story of Zhuangzi and the butterfly: "Zhuangzi dreamed that he was a butterfly and when he woke he didn't know if he was a man who dreamed he was a butterfly or was a butterfly now dreaming it was a man." Earlier, Socrates had asked the same question to one of his bewildered disciples: "How can you determine whether at this moment we are sleeping, and all our thoughts are a dream, or whether we are awake, and talking to one another?" Alice faces an even more terrifying conundrum in Tweedledee and Tweedledum's wood, where the Red King is lying asleep at the foot of a tree and (according to Tweedledee) dreaming of her. "If that there King," says Tweedledum, "was to wake, you'd go out—bang!—just like a candle!" The Italian writer Giovanni Papini borrowed the same conceit in his story "The Sick Gentleman's Last Visit." Segismundo in Calderón's *Life Is a Dream* does not know how to distinguish between waking life and dream life, though his audience does, and Segismundo must wait for hard reality to teach him the difference. Hamlet's doubts are the same as Segismundo's, but expressed in reverse: bad dreams are what let Hamlet know that he is not bounded in a nutshell, counting himself a king of infinite space.

The apparent confusion between the reality of dreams and the reality of waking life (like the confusion between madness and dreams which Socrates noted in the same dialogue) allows writers to use dreams to question reality without having to attempt an impossible imitation of a dreamlike state. The brilliant Romanian novelist Norman Manea, in *The Hooligan's Return*, notes a dream in which the autobiographical protagonist, exiled to New York, discovers that everyone in the street—taxi drivers, passersby, policemen—speaks Romanian. The dream has lent the exile's reality the quality of paradise lost. Because paradise, like dreams, is always conceived as irredeemably vanished or unrequitedly desired, the literary depictions of paradise and of dreams share a keen perception of that which is true and yet impossible. In one of his unpublished notebooks, Coleridge wrote: "If a man could pass through Paradise in a dream, and have a flower presented to him as a pledge that his soul had really been there, and if he found that flower in his hand when he awoke—Aye! and what then?" So unanswerable is the question, so neatly does it blend the reality of dreams and the reality of waking life, that H. G. Wells, in order to lend verisimilitude to the nightmare fantasy of *The Time Machine*, borrowed Coleridge's unsettling supposition and concluded his story with just such a flower.

In literature, dreams often serve to bring the impossible into the fabric of everyday life, like mist through a crack in the wall. Unfortunately, it often happens that dreams are brought in as an alibi for the unbelievable plot, and the device fails through the writer's ineptitude. A number of supernatural stories conclude with this cop-out: "It was all a dream!" In the best of cases, the reader is simply not convinced; in the worst, the conclusion dilutes whatever power the story might have held in its own right. Kafka reversed the procedure to great effect: it is not the dream but real life that proves to be Gregor's nightmare when he wakes up from disturbing dreams to find himself transformed into a monstrous insect. Dostoyevsky used a different method: to lend his story a feeling of anguish and unease, he had one of the characters in *The Possessed* tell his beloved of a dream that has the whiff of a place somewhat like hell: "Last night I dreamed that you led me into a place inhabited by a spider the size of a man, and that we spent the rest of our lives watching it in terror."

Hell, however, is not a place propitious for dreaming: Dante emerges from the "dark wood" "full of sleep" and once in Hell he faints, or slumbers, but does not dream. Purgatory is another matter. In Purgatory, Dante has three dreams. Close to the Gate of Purgatory, at the hour when "our mind, more like a pilgrim from the flesh and less captive to thoughts, is in its vision almost divine," Dante has a dream. He is whisked away, like Ganymede, by an eagle who bears him up to sun, where they both burst into flames. Then Dante wakes, to find that he has indeed been transported, not by an eagle but by Saint Lucy, his protector. The dream has told him that which truly has taken place. Later, as morning approaches in the Cornice of the Slothful, Dante falls asleep and dreams of a woman, "stammering, with eyes asquint and crooked on her feet, with maimed hands, and of sallow hue." She begins to sing, and says she is the "sweet Siren who tempts sailors in the high seas," and Dante cannot draw his eyes from her. When he awakes, Virgil tells him that she is the "ancient witch" who has brought sorrow to the world, and he must learn to free himself from her. Finally, after crossing the Wall of Fire and not far from the Garden of Eden, again at daybreak, Dante has his third dream. A young lady is gathering flowers and singing. She says her name is Leah, sister of Rachel who "never leaves her mirror and sits all day." With this, Dante wakes. All three dreams are obviously allegorical, but they are also dreams within the greater dream of the entire *Commedia*. They are deliberately artificial; they have almost nothing of the psychological shades and tangible detail of Dante's account of the journey. They stand as counterpoints to the reality of the rest of the enthralling fantasy, to highlight the "not false errors" with things that "give false matter for doubting." Literary dreams, for Dante, are the contrary of fictional accounts: they mustn't try to be convincing except as fantasies, or to be believed except as fables. To dream is for Dante equivalent to reading stories.

Perhaps here is a clue to the links between the dreams of real life and the dreams of literature. Dante, we assume, has undertaken his great voyage through the three realms of the Otherworld and returned before he writes the poem by means of which we too can undertake the same journey. Because of the intensity of the poem, we are likely to forget that our path through the *Commedia* is a retracing of Dante's steps, a second passing, as it were, laid over the first one, an imperfect transcription because much of what Dante has undergone and seen is beyond the realm of words. And so we have the *Commedia* as a translation or extended metaphor of the original experience, a "transport to another place," which is the etymological meaning of both *translation* and *metaphor*.

But what is this "original experience"? Borges observed that it is inexact to call Dante's poem a vision because a vision is a sudden revelation, fully realized in the instant of perception, and the *Commedia* extends through the one hundred cantos in a progression of learning and experience. Rather than a vision, Dante's voyage has the quality of a dream. And yet, what we read—the chronicle of a voyage—is too carefully wrought, too detailed to reflect a dreamlike state. If the original is a dream, then the poem is the improved recounting of that dream, and both the meticulous narrative and the spaces of ineffability are fully justified, even demanded, in a narrative that aspires to and indeed succeeds in being utterly believable. This is the truth declared by Dante when, before describing the appearance of the monster of fraud, Geryon, he tells us that he swears by the truth of the verses of the poem we are reading. In this vertiginous spiral we are caught as we reach the very middle of Hell: the dream of the voyage is true because the account of the dream of the voyage is true—the fiction of words supporting the fiction of the dreams of reason.

A few days after having written in his notebook about the impossibility of narrating dreams, Hawthorne made another entry: "A dream, the other night, that the world has become dissatisfied with the inaccurate manner in which facts are reported, and had employed me, with a salary of a thousand dollars, to relate things of public importance exactly as they happen." Surely, Hawthorne was aware of the wonderful paradox of having a dream, a state which he earlier described as impossible to relate precisely, engaging him to report events "exactly as they happen"—and at a salary of a thousand dollars, no less, a vast sum in the mid-nineteenth century. Perhaps this was Hawthorne's way (or the way of Hawthorne's dreams) of admitting the truth about the writer's so-called craft: that it consists of a morbid compulsion to make up stories in order to acknowledge our human condition, in spite of knowing that his instrument is unreliable, his perception of things blurred, his understanding of the world muddled, and his reliance on the reader's goodwill often unjustified.

In the nineteenth book of the *Odyssey*, Penelope speaks of dreams and says that they come forth through two gates: one made of burnished ivory, for the dreams that deceive us, and one of glistening horn, for the dreams that tell us the truth. Perhaps writers must content themselves with using only the ivory gate to chronicle their dreams, truly dreamt or invented, and yet knowing that their craft consists in telling lies. Except that the lies told by writers are not untruths; they are merely not real. In Dante's words, "Not false errors." The distinction is important.

EVER SINCE I LEARNED THE ALPHABET, THE COM-
plicated art of distinguishing between factual untruths
and "not false errors" was first taught to me through
words. Later, when I encountered the material experiences of lying and making things up, I found that I had
the words to name them both. Words are our (however
feeble) guide to what is treason and what is true.

Perhaps that is why one of my favorite sections in the
library (now in a carefully labeled box) is the one that
housed my dictionaries. For my generation (I was born
in the first half of the previous century) dictionaries mattered. Our elders treasured their Bible, or the complete
works of Shakespeare, or Betty Crocker's cookbook, or
the six volumes of the Lagarde-Michard. For the generations of this third millennium, the beloved object may

not be a book at all—perhaps a nostalgic Gameboy or an iPhone. But for many readers of my age, Petit Robert, Collins, Sopena, and Webster's were the names of our libraries' guardian angels. Mine, when I was in high school, was the Spanish edition of the *Petit Larousse Illustré,* with its pink stratum of foreign phrases separating common words from proper names.

In the days of my youth, for those of us who liked to read, the dictionary was a magical object of mysterious powers. In first place, because we were told that here, in this small fat volume, was almost the entirety of our common language, that between the drab covers were all the words that named everything in the world that we knew and also everything in the world that we did not know, that the dictionary held the past (all those words spoken by our grandparents and great-grandparents, mumbled in the dark, which we no longer used) and the future (words to name what we might one day want to say, when a new experience would call for them). In second place, because the dictionary, like a benevolent Sibyl, answered all our questions when we stumbled over difficult words in a story (even though, as Helen Keller's teacher complains in *The Miracle Worker,* "What use is a dictionary if you have to know how a word is spelled before you can find out how to spell it?").

In school, we were taught to be curious. Whenever we asked a teacher what something meant, we were told to "look it up in the dictionary!" We never thought of this as a punishment. On the contrary: with this command we were given the keys to a magic cavern in which one word would lead without rhyme or reason (except an arbitrary alphabetical reason) to the next. We would look up *poudroie*, for example, after reading in *La Barbe Bleue* (Blue Beard), "Je ne vois rien que le Soleil qui poudroie, et l'herbe qui verdoie" (I see nothing but the dust-raising Sun and the grass shining green), and discover not only the sense in which Charles Perrault used the word but that, in Canada (a name that for me was still nothing but a vast pink shape on the map), *poudroyer* meant "être chassée par le vent (souvent en rafales), en parlant de la neige," referring to snow, being chased by the wind (often in gusts). And farther down on the same page, this exquisite term, "Poudrin: pluie fine et glacée, à Terre-Neuve": In Newfoundland, light and icy rain. Several decades later, when caught in an icy downpour in Saint John's, Newfoundland, I found that I had the word to name the experience. Aby Warburg, the great reader, defined for us all what he called a library's "law of the good neighbor." According to Warburg, the book with which one was familiar was not, in most cases, the book one needed. It was the unknown neighbor on the same shelf that contained the vital information. The same can be said of the words in a dictionary. In the electronic age, however, a virtual dictionary offers perhaps less chance for serendipity, or for the kind of happy distraction which filled Émile Littré with such pride: "Many times," Littré reported, "it happened that, looking up a certain word, I became so interested that I would continue reading the next definition and then the next, as if I were holding in my hands an ordinary book."

These magical properties were probably unsuspected that singular hot afternoon, almost three thousand years ago, when somewhere in Mesopotamia an inspired and anonymous ancestor of ours scratched in a piece of clay a slim list of Akkadian words and their meanings, thus creating what must have been, to all effects and purposes, a dictionary. For a dictionary designed much along the lines of ours today, we had to wait until the first century, when Pamphilus of Alexandria put together the earliest Greek lexicon with the words in alphabetical order. Did Pamphilus intuit that among his descendants would be swarms of illustrious lexicographers toiling in languages not yet born?

Sebastián de Covarrubias in Spain, Émile Littré in France, Dr. Johnson in England, Noah Webster in the States: their names became synonymous with their scholarly creations. Today we speak of fetching a Langenscheidt or a Sopena, or of consulting a *calepin*, after the Italian Ambrogio Calepino put together, in 1502, a gigantic multilingual dictionary worthy of the Epiphany. I remember once, at the house of a friend in the Gaspé in French Canada, discussing whether the word *névé* (which appears in a novel by Erckmann-Chatrian and means "un amas de neige durci," a heap of hard snow) came from Quebec. My friend called out to his wife: "*Chérie*, bring Béslisle to the table!" as if inviting the learned Louis-Alexandre Béslisle himself, author of the *Dictionnaire général de la langue française au Canada*, to share our dinner. I believe this familiarity says something important about the nature of a reader's relationship with dictionaries.

Eighth Digression

Dictionary makers are astonishing creatures who rejoice, above everything else, in words. In spite of Dr. Samuel Johnson's definition of a lexicographer as "a harmless drudge," dictionary makers are notoriously passionate and don't believe in social niceties insofar as their great task is concerned. Think of James Murray, mastermind behind the great *Oxford English Dictionary,* who for many years received thousands of earliest instances of English words from an American surgeon living in England whom he never met, until he discovered, with splendid indifference, that his contributor, in addition to being a talented researcher, was also a clinically insane murderer whose home was the lunatic asylum of Broadmoor. Think of Noah Webster, who was caught by his wife in the arms of the maid. "Doctor Webster," she exclaimed, "I am surprised!" "No Madam," he corrected her. "I am surprised. You are astonished." Think of Thomas Cooper, the sixteenth-century scholar, who compiled for many years an important Latin-English dictionary. When he was halfway through his work, his wife, angry at his always sitting up so late at night, crept into his study, seized all his notes and threw them in the fire. "For all that," reported the gossipy antiquarian John Aubrey, "the good man had so great a zeal for the advancement of learning, that he began it again, and went with it to that Perfection that he has left us, a most useful Work." Aubrey concludes admiringly: "He was made Bishop of Winton."

Readers of dictionaries are equally passionate. Flaubert, himself a great dictionary reader, mockingly noted in his *Dictionary of Commonplaces:* "Dictionary: Say: 'It's only good for the ignorant.'" Gabriel García Márquez, while writing *A Hundred Years of Solitude,* would start every day reading the *Diccionario de la Real Academia Española*—"whose every new edition," judged the Argentinian critic Paul Groussac, "makes you nostalgic for the previous one." Ralph Waldo Emerson read the dictionary for literary pleasure. "There is no cant in it," he said, "no excess of explanation, and it is full of suggestion, the raw material of possible poems and histories." Vladimir Nabokov found in Cambridge a secondhand edition of Vladimir Dahl's *Interpretative Dic-*

tionary of the Living Great Russian Language in four volumes, and resolved to read ten pages a day since, away from his motherland, "my fear of losing or corrupting, through alien influence, the only thing I had salvaged from Russia—her language—became positively morbid."

As Nabokov understood, the language we use is not just an instrument—however feeble, inexact, treacherous—for communicating as best we can with others. Unlike other instruments, the language that we speak defines us. Our thoughts, our ethics, our aesthetics are all, up to a point, defined by our language. Each particular language provokes or allows a certain way of thinking, elicits certain specific thoughts that come to our mind not only through but because of the language we call ours. Every translator knows that passing from one language to another is less an act of reconstruction than one of reconversion, in the profoundest sense of changing one's system of belief. No French author would ever come up with "être ou ne pas être" for "To be or not to be" any more than an English author would write "For a long time I went to bed early" for "Longtemps, je me suis couché de bonne heure." Their language, not their experience, disallows it, because though human experience is universally the same, after Babel the words we have to name that common experience are different. After all, the identity of things depends on what we call them.

It is an old, old story. After creating Adam out of "the dust of the ground" and placing him in a garden in Eden (as the second chapter of Genesis tells us), God went on to create every beast of the field and every fowl of the air, and brought them to Adam to see what he would call them; and whatever Adam called each living creature, "that was the name thereof." For centuries, scholars have puzzled over the curious task that God gave Adam. Was Adam supposed to invent names for the nameless creatures he saw? Or did the beasts and the fowl that God created indeed have God-given names, names which Adam was meant to know, and which he was to pronounce like a child seeing a dog or a dove for the very first time?

In the Judeo-Christian tradition, words are the beginning of everything. According to Talmudic commentators, two thousand years before the creation of heaven and earth, God brought into being seven essential things: his divine throne, paradise set to his right, hell to his left, the celestial sanctuary in front, a jewel with the name of the Messiah engraved upon it, a voice calling out from the darkness "Return, ye children of men!" and the Torah, written in black fire on white fire. The Torah was the first of these seven, and it was the Torah that God consulted before creating the world. With some reluctance, because it feared the sinfulness of the world's creatures, the Torah consented to the world's creation. Learning of the divine purpose, the letters of the alphabet descended from God's august crown, where they had been written with a pen of flames, and one by one the letters said to God: "Create the world through me! Create the world through me!" From the twenty-six letters, God chose *bet*, the first letter in the word *blessed*, and thus it was that through *bet* the world came into being. The commentators note that the only letter that did not put forward its claims was the modest *aleph*; to reward its humility, God later gave *aleph* the first place in the alphabet. From this ancient conviction stems the metaphor of God as author and the world as book: a book we try to read and in which we are also written.

The magical letters, capable of making up words that hold in their utterance everything that is known, became Adam's privileged inheritance, and even after the expulsion from Eden, this gift, as our libraries prove, was not taken away from him. Adam and his children continued the task of naming, either as makers or as unriddlers, as authors or as readers, in the deep-rooted belief that everything in the world is the name we give it. If that is so (and the divine author himself seems to have vouched for this) then next to the book of the world there should be another volume, a book listing the names that Adam and his progeny gave to the things in the world. And while the world in all its mystery can forgo a clear method for lending meaning to its madness, a book of the world's words, a dictionary, requires just such an order. The alphabet, invented (it seems) by the Egyptians in about 2000 B.C.E., suits this purpose perfectly.

A quarter of the world's population uses nonalphabetic

writing. China and Japan, for instance, have other methods for ordering their dictionaries. The Chinese developed three lexicographic systems: by semantic categories, by graphic components, and by pronunciation. The first Chinese dictionary we know of was assembled in the third century under the modest title *Approaching Correctness* and contained lists of synonyms arranged in nineteen semantic categories such as "Explaining Trees" and "Explaining Insects." The obvious inconvenience was that the user needed to know the meaning of the word before being able to find it in its proper semantic group. The second system allowed words to be grouped according to recurrent graphic components known as "radicals," of which there exist over five hundred. Since many are hard to recognize, a *Chart of Characters Difficult to Look Up*, arranged by the number of strokes of a character, was provided as an appendix. Finally, Chinese dictionaries can be ordered according to the rhyme of the logogram's last syllable; the earliest of these rhyming dictionaries dates from the seventh century. These surprising lexicographical methods should not surprise us. An order based on hierarchies of meaning, on similarities of trait, or on similarities of sound is doubtless as good as any other for tidying up the unruly universe.

In the alphabetical world, the conventional sequence of letters serves as the dictionary's practical underpinning. An alphabetical order is one of exquisite simplicity that avoids the tinge of hierarchy implicit in most other methods. Things listed under *A* are not more or less important than those listed under *Z*, except that, in a library, the geographical disposition sometimes has it that the *A* books on the top shelf and the *Z* ones on the bottom are less courted than their brethren in the middle sections. Jean Cocteau, with becoming parsimony, judged that a simple dictionary was enough to contain a universal library, because "every literary masterpiece is nothing but a dictionary out of order." Indeed, every book, whether or not a masterpiece, is a dictionary out of order since, in a dizzying game of mirrors, all the words used to define a given word in a dictionary must themselves be found defined in that same dictionary. If, as I said, we are the language we speak, then dictionaries are our biographies. Everything we know, everything we dream of, everything we fear or desire, every achievement and every pettiness is in a dictionary.

The term *dictionary* has blended with *encyclopedia* and now denotes not only inventories of words but thematic repertories of everything under the sun, including the sun. In my library alone, there were dictionaries of cuisine, of film, of psychoanalysis, of German literature, of astrophysics, of heresies, of forms of address, of surrealism, of Jewish religion, of opera, of phrase and fable, of the Qur'an, of birds of northern Europe, of spices, of the *Quixote*, of bookbinding terms, of Baudelaire, of clouds, of Greek and Roman mythology, of Quebecois expressions, of African art, of difficulties in French, of saints, and of devils. There is even, I believe, a *Dictionary of Imaginary Places*. But in its truest, primordial, archetypal form, a dictionary is a dictionary of words.

Because of this simple fact, because a dictionary is first and foremost a collection of the building blocks of a given language, its core identity does not depend on how it is presented. Its earliest incarnations (Pamphilus's lexicon, for instance) are not essentially different from its appearances today on screen. Whether in the guise of a scroll (in the case of Pamphilus) or an imposing set of codexes (in the case of the complete *OED*) or conjured up in electronic windows (an on-line dictionary), it is the chosen container that grants the dictionary all the characteristics, privileges, and limitations of its own particular form. In itself, a dictionary is like a Möbius strip, a self-defining object of one surface only, collecting and explaining without claiming a narrative third dimension. Only in association with a specific container does a dictionary become an ongoing sequence of definitions, or a listing of conventional signs, or the jumbled story of our language, or an almost limitless storehouse of disconnected word fragments. It is the readers who, preferring one form over another according to their own requirements and inclinations, choosing either a printed codex or a virtual text, recognize in a dictionary one or several of many books: an anthology, a hierarchical catalogue, a philological thesaurus, a parallel memory, a writing and reading tool. A dictionary is all these things, though not all perhaps at the same time.

One more question: dictionaries are catalogues of definitions, but can we trust those definitions? Novalis, in 1798, wondered how it was possible to trust words to carry the meaning of things. "Nobody knows," he wrote, "the essential characteristic of language, namely that it is only concerned with itself. If only one could make people understand that language is like a mathematical formula—it constitutes a world of its own, it simply plays with itself. And that is the very reason why the strange play of relations among things mirrors itself in language." For Novalis, the power of language is not that words define things, but that the relationship between words is like the relationship between things. A dictionary is then a collection of touchstones, marking points in an incommensurable web whose individual nature remains unknown to us but whose constellations allow us a glimpse, however brief, however slight, of the machinery of the universe where everything we lose is gathered and everything we forget is remembered.

If books are our records of experience and libraries our depositories of memory, a dictionary is our talisman against oblivion. Not a memorial to language, which smacks of the grave, or a treasury, which implies something closed and inaccessible. A dictionary, intent on recording and defining, is in itself a paradox: on one hand, accumulating that which a society creates for its own consumption, hoping for a shared comprehension of the world; on the other, circulating what it amasses so that the old words won't die on the page and new words are not left out in the cold. The Latin adage "verba volant, scripta manent" has two complementary meanings. One is that the words we speak have the power to soar, while the ones that are written remain rooted to the page, the other is that words spoken can fly away and vanish in the air, while the written words are kept tethered until called for. In practical terms, dictionaries collect our words both to preserve them and to give them back to us, to allow us to see what names we have given to our experience throughout time, and also to discard some of those names and renew them in an ongoing ritual of baptism. In this sense, dictionaries are life preservers: they confirm and invigorate the lifeblood of a language. There are, of course, historical dictionaries of terms no longer in use and dictionaries of so-called dead tongues, but even these grant their subjects a brief resurrection every time someone consults them. Borges, studying the ancient northern sagas, often looked up words in Bosworth and Toller's *Anglo-Saxon Dictionary*, and liked to recite the "Our Father" in the language of the ancient inhabitants of Britain "to give God," he said, "a little surprise."

WHEN I STARTED WRITING THESE PAGES, I IM-
agined that I had reached one of the last chapters in my
reading life. The library packed and gone, my writing
career almost over and, even though I can count on the
fingers of both hands the number of years reasonably left
to me, the hope for a quiet time of conversations with old
friends, rereading books whose voices are comfortingly
familiar, and a few last visits to places whose cartography
is part of my imaginary landscape: these were some of the
things I thought I could look forward to. However, I was
to be (in Dr. Webster's sense) surprised.

This is what happened. In spite of having unpacked
and packed up so many libraries throughout my reader's
life, I was never truly a librarian. My libraries (even the
final one in France) lacked a catalogue, the sections were

madly idiosyncratic, the order haphazard, partly alphabetical and partly due to secret reasons often forgotten,
and yet I always knew how to find a book because the
only user was myself. But as someone who had lived for
so long among books, I should have known as well that
sometimes what seems like the last chapter is only the beginning of another volume. In November 2015, I received
a message from the newly appointed minister of culture
of Argentina, offering me the position of director of the
National Library.

Argentina had been throughout my life, in an uncertain, uneasy way, part of the landscape I call mine. I was
born in Buenos Aires, but because my father was in the
diplomatic service, when I was a few months old I was
taken to his first posting and didn't return until I was
seven. I did my schooling in Buenos Aires, and left again
in 1969 as a twenty-one-year-old eager to travel. I returned
on a number of occasions, but I never lived in Argentina
again. In 2014, after my partner and I left France, we settled in New York. Now I was asked to leave everything
once more and return to Buenos Aires. After much hesita-
tion, I accepted.

The city I discovered was now, of course, another, and
I found it difficult to walk down its streets without remembering the ghosts of what had been there before, or
what my memory imagined had been there before, long
ago, during my adolescence. After so many years, Buenos

Aires felt like one of those places seen in sleep whose features seem familiar but which nevertheless keep changing, drifting away as you try to make your way through them. What hadn't changed, fortunately, was the bookish nature of the city. Many of the bookstores and bookstalls where I used to stop on my way back from school had disappeared, but several were still there, and many others had sprung up, and here too I found doppelgängers. Buenos Aires has always been a city of books, ever since its foundation. I remember the curious pride I felt when our history teacher told us that Buenos Aires had been founded with a library.

Ninth Digression

Fifteenth-century Spain, heir not only to the rhetorical intelligence of Augustine but also to his misogyny and racial
prejudices, cast its long shadow over the bloody adventures that some call the Conquest and others the Invasion of
the Americas. The literate and illiterate soldiers who sailed
for the New World carried with them not only their my-
thologies and faith—mermaids and Amazons, giants and
unicorns, the redeeming god who is nailed to a cross and
the tale of the Virgin Mother—but also the printed books
in which these stories were recorded or retold. It is moving
to discover that in Christopher Columbus's account of his
first voyage across the Atlantic, upon reaching the coast of

Guinea, the admiral saw three manatees swimming close to his ship and wrote that he saw "three mermaids emerge quite visibly from the sea, but," he added with commendable honesty, "they are not as beautiful as they are made out to be." Antonio Pigafetta, who traveled with Magellan on his voyage around the world, described the inhabitants of the southernmost part of the continent as big-footed or "patagones" because he thought he recognized in the tall natives dressed in boots and capes of fur the biblical Nephilim, the offspring of the gods and of the daughters of men mentioned in the book of Genesis. Francisco de Orellana gave the river and the jungle of the land he explored the name "Amazon" because in the women warriors he and his men encountered, Orellana recognized the legendary tribe described by Herodotus. All these men were readers, and their books told them what they were going to see long before they saw it.

A number of these readers brought with them not only the recollection of their readings but the physical books themselves, and when these did not suffice, they began making new ones to furnish their libraries in the New World. Juan de Zumárraga, an elderly priest, was proposed by the Spanish emperor as the bishop of Mexico City. Named Protector of the Indians, Zumárraga proceeded to burn thousands of native manuscripts and artifacts that he deemed contrary to the true faith. At the same time, he encouraged the emperor to allow him to set up a printing press to provide the new converts with catechisms and manuals for confessors written in the native tongues. In a literary twist that Henry James might have enjoyed, the man responsible for the destruction of many of the earliest documents of the Olmec, Aztec, and Mayan civilizations was responsible as well for establishing, in 1539, the first printing press in all the Americas. The earliest productions of the press included a book by Zumárraga himself, *Brief Doctrine of the Christian Faith*, but also a Latin edition of the *Dialectics* of Aristotle and a handbook of Mexican (native) grammar by Alonso de Molina. Books are often wiser and more generous than their makers.

The imaginary reality of books contaminates every aspect of our life. We act and feel under the shadow of literary actions and feelings, and even the indifferent states of nature are perceived by us through literary descriptions, something John Ruskin called "the pathetic fallacy." This contamination, this style of thought, for want of a better term, allows us to believe that the world around us is a narrative world, and that landscapes and events are part of a story that we are compelled to follow at the same time that we create it. This imaginative credulity leads us to unearth Troy but also to hunt the unicorn of whom, a Chinese bestiary tells us, we know nothing because its shyness prevents it from appearing before human eyes.

Among the stories that the Spanish explorers brought to the New World were many that dealt with fabulous kingdoms such as the ones featured in the novels of chivalry, kingdoms in which Don Quixote was an ardent believer. If cities of gold and mountains of precious stones populated the geography of those brave, imaginary epics, their emulators believed that richer golden cities and higher precious mountains would certainly exist in the strange and wonderful lands that they thought were the Indies.

In 1516, the explorer Juan Díaz de Solís sailed into the River Plate, landed a handful of men on the muddy western bank, and was promptly killed and eaten by the Charrúa natives. Some of the survivors continued the voyage and sailed along the coast of Brazil to a place they called Santa Catarina, where a tribe of Tupiguaraníes told them about a mysterious White King, Lord of the Silver Mountain. According to their account, somewhere inland, deep in the jungle, there rose a mountain made entirely of pure silver. The king of that realm was known to be a generous and peace-loving monarch who would gladly give travelers part of his treasure to take away as a sign of goodwill. One of the survivors, Alejo García, decided to mount an expedition to search for the fabulous kingdom. García managed to cross the vast green continent and reach the heights of Peru. He was killed by native arrows on his return journey, but his men brought back with them to Santa Catarina a few chunks of silver ore, presumably from the area of Potosí, that were offered as proof of the truth of the story. From then on, the Conquest of the New World was fired by the belief that a magical realm of marvelous riches lay far in the interior of the continent, ready for the picking.

Alejo García died in 1525. Ten years later, in 1535, an aristocratic knight, Pedro de Mendoza, who had served as chamberlain to the emperor and fought in Italy against the French, became convinced that he was the man to find the White King and dispossess him of his riches. Mendoza launched an expedition of thirteen ships and two thousand men, partly funded by himself and partly by the emperor Charles I, who stipulated that Mendoza set up three Spanish fortified towns on the conquered land and, within two years, transport a thousand Spanish colonists to inhabit them. However, after they crossed the Atlantic, a terrible storm scattered Mendoza's fleet off the coast of Brazil. Natural catastrophes are often mirrored by human ones. Shortly after the storm, Mendoza's lieutenant was mysteriously murdered. These were not the ideal conditions in which to start a colony or undertake a treasure hunt.

On the banks of the same wide and muddy river where the natives had feasted on Solís, on 2 February 1536 Mendoza founded a city he called Nuestra Señora Santa María del Buen Ayre after the patroness of Sardinia, a name that successive centuries would trim down to Buenos Aires. Mendoza suffered from syphilis and his intermittently confused state of mind was not conducive to an effective government. Five years later, due to Mendoza's failings and to the belligerence of the indigenous population, the city was abandoned. It was to be founded again some forty-two years later by Juan de Garay. In 1537, a sick and wretched man, Mendoza attempted to return to Spain but died on the homeward journey.

Among the crew of Mendoza's expedition was the twenty-five-year-old son of a wealthy German merchant, Ulrich Schmidl. Schmidl was witness to the degradation and collapse of the new city, and to the struggles of the colonizers to survive under the constant attacks of the native population. After the city was abandoned, he traveled up to what is today Paraguay and was present at the founding of another city, Asunción, and then traveled farther, to today's Bolivia. Receiving news that his elder brother had died and that he had inherited the family fortune, Schmidl asked for a discharge and returned to Europe in 1552. There he wrote an account of his experiences, based on a detailed journal he had kept throughout his adventures. The book was published in Frankfurt in 1557 under the imposing title *True History of a Remarkable Voyage Undertaken by Ulrich Schmidl of Straubing in America or the New World, from 1534 to 1554, Where Can Be Found All of His Misfortunes of Nineteen Years as Well as a Description of the Lands and Noteworthy People He Saw There, Written by Himself.* Several translations quickly followed, in Latin, French, and Spanish.

Schmidl's account, the first of what can be called the history of Argentina, chronicles in lurid detail the atrocious conditions of the life of Mendoza's men. Under siege by the indigenous population, the colonists starved, eventually resorting to cannibalism: as soon as one of them was hanged for treason or a petty crime, the others hacked the body to pieces and ate it. Schmidl sheds a different light on the European conception of the cannibal savages by documenting the fact that Europeans too were capable of such acts. Montaigne, in an influential essay written at about the same time as Schmidl's chronicle, using cannibalism as his point of departure, attempted to subvert the notion of European superiority. Montaigne had met one of these "cannibals," brought to France from the Americas by a French expedition, and had in his employ a servant who had spent many years living among them. These cannibals, Montaigne wrote, were not the savages Europeans imagined but people who lived harmoniously, respected the nature that surrounded them, and possessed all manner of technical and artistic skills. They held solid religious beliefs and lived under a perfectly efficient form of government, unlike Montaigne's fellow Frenchmen. These so-called savages, Montaigne pointed out, had no slaves, no rich and no poor; they spoke a language in which the words for treason and lying, envy and avarice were absent. If the stories of Greece and Rome, and the literature of chivalry, had fed the explorers' imagination before they came to the New World, as a foreword to what they would see, Schmidl and Montaigne's accounts colored the vision of the Americas in the decades that followed as an afterword to the immense saga.

Mendoza had brought with him a small collection of books that in a secret way may define the city that he had imagined. Perhaps all cities are founded with a library in mind. The books Mendoza brought with him were "seven volumes of a medium size bound in black leather," whose titles, unfortunately, have not come down to us. He also brought with him a book by Erasmus, "also medium-sized and bound in the same black leather," a collection of Petrarch's poems, a "little book with golden covers that says inside 'Virgil,'" and a volume by De Bridia bound in vellum. It seems that C. de Bridia (we only know the initial of his first name) was a Franciscan monk who accompanied the mission of John of Plano Carpini to Mongolia in 1247 and wrote a detailed history of the Mongol people titled *Tartar Relation*—a manuscript that is now in the Beinecke Library at Yale University.

This modest list is wonderfully revealing. The books that Mendoza brought with him to found Buenos Aires tell us of an eclectic, generous conception (probably unconscious, certainly not explicit) of what this new city should be. In this founding library we find: a philosopher of a faith that was not Mendoza's own (Erasmus), poets in tongues other than Spanish (Petrarch and Virgil because Mendoza's education would have included Latin), a fellow explorer from another age and another culture—the far north of Tartary, as opposed to the far south of the New World. For Pedro de Mendoza, contemporary of Alonso Quijano, the world of the intellect was all one, or, in other words, any singular undertaking formed part of a universal whole. Symbolically, if not deliberately, the impulse to bring with him these books lends the identity of the city yet to be imaginative power and a sort of immortal persona.

THE NATIONAL LIBRARY I HAD KNOWN IN THE 1960s had been a different one. It stood in the colonial neighborhood of Boedo, on Mexico Street, an elegant nineteenth-century palazzo built to house the state lottery but almost immediately converted into a library. Borges had kept his office there on the first floor, after he was appointed director in 1955, when "God's irony," he said, simultaneously granted him "the books and the night": Borges was the fourth blind director of the library (a curse I'm intent on avoiding). It was in this building that for several years I used to meet Borges after school, and walk him back to his flat, where I would read for him stories by Kipling, Henry James, Stevenson. I associate that library with those stories.

The library I now discovered, half a century later, was lodged in a gigantic tower designed by the architect Clorindo Testa in the brutalist style of the sixties. Borges, passing his hands over the architect's model, dismissed it as "a hideous sewing machine." The building is supposed to represent a book lying on a tall cement table, but people call it the UFO, an alien thing landed among luscious gardens and blue jacaranda trees. It is a vast vertical labyrinth of cement and glass, seven stories high and three stories below ground, and includes several adjacent buildings as well. Close to a thousand people work there.

The previous administration had concentrated its efforts on political and popular events which effectively raised the visibility of the institution, especially within the city of Buenos Aires. However, it had paid less attention to the technical aspects of the library, such as bringing the catalogue up to date and extending the digitizing programs, so when I took up my appointment I was not able to tell with any accuracy how many books the library held in its stacks. "Between three and five million" was the closest guess.

At the beginning of my term, the library did not have an explicit strategic plan or even an articulated set of institutional goals: these were some of the things that I was keen to develop. At the start, much of the work proved to be purely administrative. I felt like those characters in a Jules Verne novel who find themselves on some faraway island and have to conjure up survival skills they never knew they had. I made it my priority to reorganize a number of different sections of the library so that work could become more efficient and coherent. I tried to do this in several ways—for instance, by setting up Press and Communications under one head instead of two, grouping together the various areas of Acquisitions and Donations, restructuring the Cultural Programming as well as the Research Department, and giving areas such as the Library Archives the room they badly needed. Above all, it was essential to establish a work schedule that would ensure that the catalogue be brought up to date and that a list of priorities for the Digitization Department be established to allow us to accept commissions from the provincial libraries of Argentina. Attempting to do all this, I felt that I was paying an old debt to my abandoned library so haphazardly organized, so dependent on my personal energy and whim, a microcosmic model of the huge colossus inside which I now found myself. Old sins cast long shadows.

The National Library, as an autarchic federal institution, is supposed to be the library of all the people of Argentina, but up to recently it had served mostly the readers of the city of Buenos Aires. Shortly after my arrival, I started traveling across the country in order to get to know the provincial librarians, find out what their needs were, and establish agreements to encourage common projects. These

trips allowed me to make astonishing discoveries, sometimes the single copy of a rare book squirreled away in a
remote corner, sometimes whole archives of precious material, such as the collection of travelers' accounts held in
the Library of the End of the World in Tierra del Fuego, all
evidence of the impulse we have, as a species, to collect
and store and preserve.

Borges had imagined the National Library of Argentina, sub specie aeternitatis, as universal. With this in
mind, I began to sign agreements with other national libraries and several university libraries from around the
world, hoping that these agreements might lead to joint
exhibitions and seminars, the exchange of librarians and
researchers, the sharing of digital collections and general
assistance for one another in a number of other ways.
Robert Darnton, the former director of the Harvard University Library, imagined a common digital library that
would assemble the holdings of the university libraries
of the United States; perhaps in the future we can plan,
along similar lines, a universal digital library.

In my adolescence, no doubt under the influence of
Borges, I tried to write a few fantastic stories, now fortunately lost. One of them, I remember, was about an
unbearable know-it-all to whom the devil, in exchange
for I don't recall what, entrusted the overseeing of the
world. Suddenly, this oaf realizes that he has to deal with
everything at once, from the rising of the sun to the turn-

ing of every page, from the falling of every leaf to the coursing of each drop of blood in every vein. Obviously, the know-it-all is crushed by the inconceivable immensity of the task. Without indulging in such an overwhelming ambition, ever since my first books I had wanted to try to put my ideas about reading and libraries into action. Now I got my wish with a vengeance. From one day to the next, I have become an accountant, technician, lawyer, architect, electrician, psychologist, diplomat, sociologist, specialist in union politics, technocrat, cultural programmer, and, of course, administrator of actual library matters. But in my particular case, what does being a library director mean?

Here I must turn back to an earlier chapter. In 1982, I moved with my family to Canada. A few years later, I applied for Canadian citizenship. This was because I felt, for the first time in my nomadic life, that I was in a society where I could have an active role as a citizen. Not only could I vote and add my name to a census, but more importantly I could try to change the national, provincial, and municipal rules and regulations by taking a responsible part in the public discourse. I could do this in a number of ways: by becoming a member of associations such as the Writers' or the Translators' Union, by forming part of school boards, by taking on jury duties at the Ontario Arts Council and the Arts Council of Canada, by sitting on official committees, and by appearing on national radio and television, and in the printed press. For the first time in my life, I, the Wandering Jew, felt something like civic responsibility.

Now I was back in Argentina, where a number of questions sprang to mind. Why is it that in the majority of our societies, citizens lack an effective political voice? Why does a citizen have to react against acts of injustice either by turning a blind eye or by resorting to stolid violence? Why are most of our societies so weak in what we might call civic ethics? And more important for me, can a national library, as a central symbol of a society's identity, serve as a source for learning the vocabulary of civic ethics and as a workshop for its practice?

I believe that at the root of these questions lies a certain idea of justice. When an individual feels that an act is unjust and reacts against it from what he or she thinks is just, the source of both the feeling and the reaction is often a communal and primal notion of what is fair or unfair. And where is this communal notion of fairness better expressed, better recorded, than in our public libraries?

Tenth Digression

For reasons that are still mysterious and which, perhaps, if revealed, might seem banal, in the eighth year C.E. the poet Publius Ovidius Naso was banished from Rome by the emperor Augustus. Ovid (his three names reduced to one by centuries of devoted readers) ended his days in a backwater village on the west coast of the Black Sea, pining for Rome. He had been at the heart of the heart of the empire which, in those days, was synonymous with the world; to be banished was for Ovid like a death sentence, because he could not conceive of life outside his beloved city. According to Ovid himself, at the root of the imperial punishment was a poem. We don't know what the words of that poem were, but they were powerful enough to terrify an emperor.

Since the beginning of time (the telling of which is also a story) we have known that words are dangerous creatures. In Babylon, in Egypt, in ancient Greece, the person capable of inventing and recording words, the writer, whom the Anglo-Saxons called "the maker," was thought to be the darling of the gods, a chosen one on whom the gift of writing had been bestowed. According to Socrates, in a legend which he either retold or imagined, the art of writing was the creation of the Egyptian god Theuth, who also invented mathematics, astronomy, checkers, and dice. In offering his invention to the pharaoh, Theuth explained that his discovery provided a recipe for memory and wisdom. But the pharaoh wasn't convinced: "What you have discovered," he said, "is not a recipe for memory but a tool to help us remember. And it is not true wisdom that you offer your disciples, but only its semblance, for by telling them of many things without teaching them, you will make them seem to know much, while for the most part they know nothing, and are filled not with wisdom but with the conceit of wisdom."

Ever since, writers and readers have debated whether literature effectively achieves anything in a society—that is to say, if literature has a role in the making of a citizen. Some, agreeing with Theuth, believe that we can learn from literature, sharing the experience of our predecessors, be-

coming wise through the memory of centuries of knowledge. Others, agreeing with the pharaoh, say with W. H.
Auden that "poetry makes nothing happen," that the memory preserved in writing does not inspire wisdom, that we
learn nothing through the imagined word, and that times of
adversity are proof of writing's failure.

It is true that, confronted with the blind imbecility with
which we try to destroy our planet, the relentlessness with
which we inflict pain on ourselves and others, the extent
of our greed and cowardice and envy, the arrogance with
which we strut among our fellow living creatures, it is hard
to believe that writing—literature or any other art, for that
matter—teaches us anything. If after reading lines such as
Larkin's "The trees are coming into leaf, / Like something
almost being said," we are still capable of all such atrocities,
then perhaps literature does make nothing happen.

In at least one sense, however, all literature is civic action: because it is memory. All literature preserves something which otherwise would die away with the flesh and
bones of the writer. Reading is reclaiming the right to this
human immortality, because the memory of writing is all-
encompassing and limitless. Individually, humans can remember little: even extraordinary memories such as that of
Cyrus, king of the Persians, who could call every soldier
in his armies by name, are nothing compared to the volumes that fill our libraries. Our books are accounts of our
histories: of our epiphanies and our atrocities. In that sense

all literature is testimonial. But among the testimonies are reflections on those epiphanies and atrocities, words that offer the epiphanies for others to share, and words that surround and denounce the atrocities so they are not allowed to take place in silence. They are reminders of better things, of hope and consolation and compassion, and hold the implication that of these too, we are all of us capable. Not all of these we achieve, and none of these we achieve all the time. But literature reminds us that they are there, these human qualities, following our horrors as certainly as birth succeeds death. They too define us.

Of course, literature may not be able to save anyone from injustice, or from the temptations of greed or the miseries of power. But something about it must be perilously effective if every dictator, every totalitarian government, every threatened official tries to do away with it, by burning books, by banning books, by censoring books, by taxing books, by paying mere lip-service to the cause of literacy, by insinuating that reading is an elitist activity. William Blake, speaking about Napoleon in a public address, had this to say: "Let us teach Buonaparte, and whosoever else it may concern, that it is not Arts that follow and attend upon Empire, but Empire that attends and follows the Arts." Napoleon was not listening then, and minor Napoleons are not listening today. In spite of thousands of years of experience, the Napoleons of this world have not learned that their methods are ultimately ineffective, and the literary imagination cannot be annihilated because it is that imagination, and not the imagination of greed, that is the surviving reality. Augustus may have exiled Ovid because he thought (and was probably not mistaken) that something in the poet's work accused him. Every day, somewhere in the world, someone attempts (sometimes successfully) to stifle a book which plainly or obscurely sounds a warning. And again and again, empires fall and literature continues. Ultimately, the imaginary places writers and their readers invent—in the etymological sense of "to come upon," "to discover"— persist because they are simply what we should call reality, because they are the real world revealed under its true name. The rest, as we should have realized by now, is merely shadow without substance, the stuff of nightmares, and it will vanish without a trace in the morning.

In the second part of *Don Quixote*, the Duke tells Sancho that, as governor of the Island of Barataria, he must dress the part: "half as a man of letters and half as a military captain, because in this island which I bestow upon you arms are as necessary as letters and letters as arms." In saying this, the Duke not only refutes the classical dichotomy but also defines the obligatory concerns of every governor, if we understand the one to mean action and the other reflection. Our actions must be justified by our literature and our literature must bear witness to our actions. Therefore to act as citizens, in times of peace as in times of war, is in some sense an extension of our reading, since our books hold the possibility of guiding us through the experience and knowledge of others, allowing us the intuition of the uncertain future and the lesson of an immutable past.

Essentially we haven't changed since the beginning of our histories. We are the same erect apes that a few million years ago discovered in a piece of rock or wood instruments of battle, while at the same time stamping on cave walls bucolic images of daily life and the revelatory palms of our hands. We are like the young Alexander, who on the one hand dreamt of bloody wars of conquest and on the other always carried with him Homer's books, which spoke of the suffering caused by war and the longing for Ithaca. Like the Greeks, we allow ourselves to be governed by sick and greedy individuals for whom death is unimportant because it happens to others, and in book after book we attempt to put into words our profound conviction that it should not be so.

For Plato, justice was the quality shared by every area of society when that society is ruled by reason; that is to say, justice considered not as a separate value in itself (such as wisdom or courage) but as an attribute shared by all these values individually. If we take justice then, in the Platonic sense, as the shared value aspired to by human society, then perhaps a national library, intended to gather all the manifestations of a particular society, could define itself as the storehouse of every kind of manifestation of justice, as a catalogue of examples of just acts (as well as unjust, of course) to instruct and remind and guide readers in their civic roles. One example must suffice. In Sophocles' play *Ajax*, when the goddess Athena gleefully tells Odysseus, her protégé, that Ajax, his foe, has been defeated through hideous sufferings, Odysseus speaks a few words which suddenly render the Greek hero far more noble than the wise and bloodthirsty goddess: "The unfortunate man might well be my enemy, and yet I pity him when I see him weighed down with misfortune. Indeed, it is towards myself more than towards him that I direct my thoughts, since I see clearly that we are, all of us who live upon this earth, nothing but ghosts or weightless shadows." I would place this paragraph on the very first page of every society's constitution.

I HAVE SAID THAT INSTITUTIONS SUCH AS A NA-
tional library carry a projected communal identity both
for those who are, in practical terms, familiar with them
and for those who are not, readers and nonreaders alike.
If a national library is to be an institution seen by the majority as central to the nation's identity (and therefore central to the civic instruction of its citizens) then a number
of conditions must apply.

A national library must be open to everyone who wishes
to use it, and it must change to fit its users' changing needs.
John Rawls distinguishes between "freedom" and "freedom's worth," that is to say, the nominal right to freedom
and the right to act according to that freedom. One could
apply this reasoning to "freedom to read" and the acting

on that freedom. Negative freedom (answering the question "What is allowed to me?") might correspond to the Alexandrian kings' ambition to collect everything, reflected today in the vast scope of the Web, collecting facts, opinions, information and misinformation, and even deliberate lies "because everything should be allowed to me." This "freedom," partial at best, is largely illusory because it doesn't entail the enablement to act on this freedom.

To be an active institution, a national library must find ways to form new users and to maintain those who already profit from its services. A just society, an ethical society comprises of course all citizens, whether they be readers or not. Statistically, we know that readers—especially readers capable of an illuminating, creative reading—constitute a very small percentage of the total number of citizens. "No one who can read," says Dickens in *Our Mutual Friend*, "ever looks at a book, even unopened on a shelf, like one who cannot." How is a national library to become capable of serving someone who doesn't look at a book in the same way as someone who can read? How can a national library convert nonreaders into readers? How can it transform the perception that most nonreaders have of libraries as alien places and books as alien instruments into a cartography in which all share a common, effective intellectual space?

I believe that to attempt to fulfill these needs, a national library must establish methods by which all citizens are made aware of the importance of reading, first as a basic skill, second as a way to stimulate and free the imagination. I have little confidence in the official reading programs I have seen in Canada, or in many other countries. Essentially, most of these programs follow methods borrowed from the advertising world, whereby popular figures, such as a film star or a sports icon, are shown in the act of reading, and free books are distributed in the streets. These methods are supposed to create consumers. They don't. The only proven method by which a reader is born is one that, to my knowledge, has not yet been discovered. In my experience, what occasionally does work (not always) is the example of a passionate reader. Sometimes the experience of a friend, a parent, a teacher, a librarian obviously moved by reading a certain page can inspire, if not immediate imitation, at least curiosity. And that, I think, is a good beginning. The discovery of the art of reading is intimate, obscure, secret, almost impossible to explain, akin to falling in love, if you will forgive the maudlin comparison. It is acquired by oneself alone, like a sort of epiphany, or perhaps by contagion, confronted by other readers. I don't know of many more ways. The happiness procured by reading, like any happiness, cannot be enforced. When Diodorus Siculus visited Egypt in the first century B.C.E., he saw engraved on the entrance to the ruins of an ancient library an inscription: "Clinic of the Soul." Perhaps that can be a library's ultimate aspiration.

However, to allow actual or potential readers to see the library as a place of their own, a national library must not only hold but be seen to hold material corresponding to the imagination of all segments of the population. In the National Library of Argentina, I discovered that while some effort had been made to collect material related to the victims of the military dictatorship of the seventies (a task undertaken on a vaster scale by the Centro Cultural de la Memoria "Haroldo Conti" in Buenos Aires, established in 2004), almost nothing had been done in a focused way regarding native communities, gay, lesbian, and transgender histories, and the feminist movement in Argentina. We have now begun to assemble material in these areas and to provide improved descriptions and access to existing holdings. "The world," wrote the Austrian poet Ilse Aichinger, "is made of that which demands to be observed." This is our justification.

A national library must also be the custodian of the facts and records of our experience of the world. "A library is about evidence," Richard Ovenden, director of the Bodleian Library, once told me. To fulfill this role, a national library must guarantee the availability of points of reference (*repères*) in its holdings which might enable those who seek them to ask better questions and imagine new social models more just and more equitable. The evolutionary biologist Marc Hauser has suggested that all human beings share a "universal moral grammar," hardwired into our neural pathways, and manifested in our artistic output. Scientific studies such as Hauser's have concluded what readers have long known: literature, better than life, provides an education in ethics and allows for the growth of empathy, essential to engage in the social contract. Perhaps the art of telling stories developed as an instrument to assert this human quality, a quality that plays such an essential part in our intellectual and social lives. We know from Darwinian studies that empathy evolved into a fundamental trait for human survival almost as soon as our earliest ancestors began to interact, helping one another and working in common pursuits. According to the paleoanthropologist Richard Leakey, "We are human because our ancestors learned to share their food and their skills in an honored network of obligation." Out of our need to work together, to develop better skills in order to explore distant horizons, empathy became an incentive to our natural curiosity. Noam Chomsky has argued further that the consumer cultures in which we now live prevent us from manifesting this empathy by attributing negative values to the understanding of and concern for the pain of others. In order to consume the worthless gadgets increasingly offered by the marketplace, the consumer has to become less an engaged citizen and more a self-centered individual, embracing the politics of egotism proposed by Ayn Rand, who in her unfortunately popular novels affirmed that "the question isn't who is going to let me; it's who is going to stop me"—a shadow version of Rawls's "positive freedom." Perhaps a national library can act as a school for empathy, transforming Borges's nightmarish universal library of Babel, filled with every possible combination of letters and therefore with almost no readable texts, into a library that houses a universal moral grammar, set out in the countless examples of moral justice in our literatures. "To change the world, Sancho my friend," says Don Quixote to his faithful companion, "is neither a utopia nor an act of madness, it's simply justice."

In a speech given at the Athenée Royale in Paris in 1819, Benjamin Constant said the following: "The purpose of the ancient world was the sharing of social power among all the citizens of a same nation: this is what they called freedom. The purpose of the modern world is the assurance of private pleasures, and they call freedom the guarantees accorded by the national institutions of such pleasures." A national library must guarantee the freedom to enjoy these pleasures—intellectual, creative, empathetic—in order that whoever wishes to can be tempted to go beyond what is offered, what is apparent, what is conventionally considered good. To reach this goal, many things are needed. Money, work, imagination, and an ongoing social dialogue, and more imagination, more work, and more money. Governments must be made to realize the importance of a national library in holding a society together as a coherent, interactive, resilient entity—and must provide the funds accordingly.

A national library can, I believe, be a sort of creative workshop, and a place in which material is stored for future readers to find clues in order to imagine better worlds. It can also be a place where new readers are formed and old readers reaffirmed. I don't know by what means we can achieve this, but I know we must try. Political pettiness, personal greed, internal squabbles, and endemic corruption all stand in the way and we must also be prepared to accept less than perfect results. As Chesterton once said, "If a thing is worth doing, it is worth doing badly."

There is an essential ineffability in any story. The digressions of which I'm over-fond say something about my story's ambiguity and irresolution, the inventions of memory try to lend it apparent coherence and order, but ultimately the shape and sense of my story escapes me. Closing down my library, packing my books, then seeing the vanished space conjured up in Lepage's magic show, and finally inconceivably becoming director of the National Library of Argentina are chapters in a narrative that I'm not able fully to grasp or understand.

There is this, however: the emptying of a library, however heartbreaking, and the packing of its books, however unjust, need not be seen as a conclusion. There are possible new orders in shadows, secret but implicit, apparent only once the old ones are taken apart. Nothing that matters is ever truly replaced. Every loss is (at least partly) for all eternity. Repetition entails variation, new questions, a certain degree of change even if much remains the same, like our features in the mirror.

Which sections of my dismantled library will survive and which will become obsolete? What unexpected alliances will be formed among my boxed volumes once housed in their future settlement? What new labels will emerge on the shelves, now that the old ones have been discarded? Will I, their customary reader, wander again through the library's stacks, pleased at recalling a title here and surprised of finding another there? Or will it be my ghost who will quietly haunt my library's next incarnation? "En ma fin gît mon commencement," "In my end is my beginning," Mary, Queen of Scots is said to have embroidered on her cloth while in prison. This seems to me a fitting motto for my library.

Acknowledgments

Over the years, many, many friends helped to maintain the library alive. They flew in from all around the world, entering the magical space of the library to read, work, talk, share books, discuss ideas. And then, in the final months, when it came time to close down, several came to catalogue the library as it had been in its prime, and organized themselves into teams to take the books off the shelves, wrap them in protective paper, place them in boxes with the appropriate labels, and make maps of where they had stood, in case I wanted to find one after they were packed because, in my mind, I'm still able to wander through the vanished library and know exactly where to find a book. I've heard that in Mennonite communities, when a barn is about to be built, friends and neighbors gather to help put up the walls and raise the roof. Here the generosity was the same, but for the contrary purpose.

Jillian Tomm, Lucie Pabel, and Gottwalt Pankow, together with Ramón de Elía and Finn Willi Zobel, were the principal dismantlers and organizers and packers, and, to assist them, they summoned several of their generous friends: Anne Frigon, Jocelyn Godolphin, Gale Hamilton, Jim Henderson, Elaine Ménard, Michael Murphy, Dominique Paquin, and Ana Simonovich among others. All this under the ever-watchful eye of Lucy, the most loving and intelligent of dogs, whose world was being so uncomprehendingly undone. I don't seem to have the right words to tell them all of my infinite debt of gratitude.

My agents Guillermo Schavelzon and Barbara Graham accompanied me faithfully through these past difficult years: to them my deepest thanks. And heartfelt thanks as well to the Yale team that waited with generous patience for the manuscript to be finished: John Donatich, my wise editor; Danielle D'Orlando, his infallible assistant; Nancy Ovedovitz, the brilliant designer who proved the falsehood of the saying about judging a book by its cover; and Susan Laity, whose Sherlockian eye has once again tracked Baskerville typos (and those in all other typefaces) across the muddy moors of my text.